RITCHIES
OF
HETTON-LE-HOLE

BOB TUCK

Published by Bob Tuck
Low Worsall, Yarm,
North Yorkshire, England TS15 9QA

ISBN 0 9521938 6 8

First Published 2005
Copyright 2005 Bob Tuck

Other books by Bob Tuck

Moving Mountains
Mountain Movers
Mammoth Trucks
Hauling Heavyweights
The Supertrucks of Scammell
Move It (Compendium of *Moving Mountains* and *Mountain Movers*)
Carrying Cargo
Classic Hauliers
Robsons
Classic Hauliers 2
The Golden Days of Heavy Haulage
A Road Transport Heritage
A Road Transport Heritage Vol II
A Road Transport Heritage Vol III
100 Years if Heavy Haulage
Trucks (reprint of *Mammoth Trucks*)
King of the Road
Hills of Botley

Printed in Great Britain by
The Amadeus Press Ltd
Cleckheaton
West Yorkshire

Typesetting by Highlight Type Bureau Ltd
Bradford, West Yorkshire

Book design by
Sylbert Productions
Pavey Ark

Front Cover: Just like Penshaw Monument in the background, the E&N Ritchie fleet of vehicles have long been a recognised part of the North East of England. Into the 21st century and the Ritchie vehicles are now being painted in a new distinctive silver livery. But as denoted by the murals painted onto the cab's side panels, the company hasn't forgotten its roots. New into service at the end of June 2005 was this Cummins powered Foden Alpha XXL 44 tonner. With long distance being the Ritchie transport arm's speciality, this vehicle will soon be a recognised sight in any part of the UK.

Rear Cover: Ritchie's first step into the mechanised world was this 1919 Crossley charabanc. In his smart uniform, regular driver Norman Ritchie is seen behind the wheel. The Crossley was to give good service but it was to be standardising on the marque of Commer that allowed Ritchies to expand. PBR 806 is now part of the Ritchie collection of finely restored vehicles and came – almost – new into service during 1960. Bought from Northern Autoport, chassis number CD 7620254 was rated as having a 10-ton capacity. Commer used the company of Unipower to convert their four wheelers into six wheelers and while many were carried out during the 1950s and '60s, not many of these vehicles have survived into preservation. With Commer TS3 two stroke engine, the Ritchie six-wheeler has been seen – and heard – on all parts of the UK rally scene.

Title Page: With gleaming Motor Panels cab, the Thornycroft Sturdy Special RPT 634 certainly looked the part on its first day at work – 3rd March 1955. With chassis no. 53405 and unladen weight of 2 tons 14cwt 2qrs (complete with body) a lot was expected from the new Ritchie vehicle. Colin Ritchie is seen getting into the cab with a full load of animal feed from Spiller's Mill in Newcastle for delivery to George Wright's, the Hetton based feed merchant. Anyone who can picture the old road from the Quayside at Newcastle, across the Swing Bridge and then all the way up through Gateshead High Street will know this is quite a testing climb. However, the brand new Sturdy Special didn't prove to be very special at all and Colin Ritchie said he hardly got out of bottom gear all the way through Gateshead. The performance of this one vehicle soured the Ritchie management so much that they decided never to buy another Thornycroft again. This was rather sad because when Jack Cook – the Thornycroft salesman – brought a brand new 1959 Mastiff demonstrator to Ritchies, Colin reckoned it was the best wagon he'd ever driven. With air brakes and power steering, it was an absolute belter, he'd apparently said. While he wanted to buy one, both Ernest and Norman disagreed – RPT 634 had been such a disaster. In fairness to the Thornycroft, it was only rated to carry 6.5 tons and no doubt Ritchies reckoned it should carry more. Its worst fault was its habit of cutting out – for no apparent reason. George Williams (who was later Foreman Mechanic at Ritchies) recalls the fault was eventually traced to a malfunctioning non-return valve – in the Thornycroft diesel engine system – but not without causing a lot of headache. The four-wheeler was put out of its agony when it was written off after tangling with a Walker Steel artic at some traffic lights in Blackburn.

Telephone   34 Hetton

E. & N. RITCHIE,
Motor Engineers and Haulage Contractors,
TRIUMPH GARAGE ✇ STATION ROAD,
HETTON-LE-HOLE,
Co. Durham.

CONTENTS

HETTON SAND & GRAVEL CO., LTD.
Registered Office.
Washed, Cubed and Graded Gravel   STATION ROAD,
and Washed Sand.   Phone : 34.   HETTON-LE-HOLE.

3

Author's acknowledgements

I suppose like many other people in the North East of England – and throughout the UK – I've been a long time observer of the E&N Ritchie transport operation, without perhaps realising how varied a history the company has seen. But to piece together that 107 years of involvement in road transport has naturally involved all manner of help from a variety of people.

She may not have realised at the time, but Carol Ritchie probably set this book going when she first sat down with Colin Ritchie – almost 18 years ago – to retrace the Ritchie family tree. Sadly Colin isn't here to reminisce about days gone by but fortunately George Kirkbride and Tom Soulsby could both still vividly recall their days at Ritchies during the 1930s and '40s. Their impressions are so strong because E&N Ritchie has always been so much a part of the closely-knit Hetton-le-Hole community.

Both Stuart and Alastair Ritchie – and their mother Sylvia - can easily recall their involvement with the business. While the view from some of the garage staff of John Smiles, George Williams, Ronnie Kirtley and Victor Last (plus Audrey Maughan from the office) has only enhanced this Ritchie story. Driver's tales of old have come from Jack Delap while with each being on the driving books for 31 years, both Malcolm 'Tucker' Carr and Jeff Sulkiewicz have also greatly helped.

Another huge source of help has been Kathleen Ecelson. She may have changed her name – with marriage – in 1958, but she still reckons she's very much a Ritchie at heart.

As relates to the physical production of this book, I've been asked to mention Dennis Tomys of Hetton Picture Framing who has slaved over some very old material to create some first class images. Of course, the quality of this book will reflect the talents of both the team from the Highlight Type Bureau and from Amadeus Press.

Last – but never least – my wife Sylvia must be mentioned. As a guide and confidant – and a continuing source of inspiration – her tireless involvement is a major factor in this book simply getting to press.

Low Worsall
June 2005
Bob Tuck

Dedication

As a family, we would like to dedicate this book to our father Colin Ritchie.

A hardworking, caring, friend and gentleman, he strove through hard times to make our lives better.

1929-1990

Foreword

We were born into the world of wagons or as they say: "It was in the blood." As a family we are very proud of our 107 years of history.

Our forefathers worked hard to establish and sustain the company through good times and bad. And it's the sheer determination of four generations of Ritchies that gives us the strength to go forward.

When Bob Tuck began writing this book, it made us realise how much we have to be proud of, as the book has brought back lots of fond memories. In truth, research of the book has also uncovered things we weren't fully aware of but it has allowed us to renew some of the memories and contacts we had left behind.

We would like to take this opportunity to thank all our staff – past and present – for all their hard work and loyalty.

We hope you all enjoy this book as much as we have enjoyed being part of it.

Triumph Garage
Hetton-le-Hole.

Stuart Ritchie
Alastair Ritchie

In 1907 (top) Ralph and his wife Alice Jane are pictured with sons Ernest (standing) and Norman. About 1956 (centre) Ernest is stood holding his grandson Stuart with his son – and Stuart's father – Colin, sporting the braces. The family gathering for the new millennium sees Alastair (centre rear row) with his hand on the shoulder of his wife Annette. Left on the back row is Nick Walton who is stood behind his wife Lynn (nee Ritchie) with their two children Lucy and Amy (sat at front). Stuart is stood at the right on the back row behind his wife Carol and their son David.

RITCHIE FAMILY

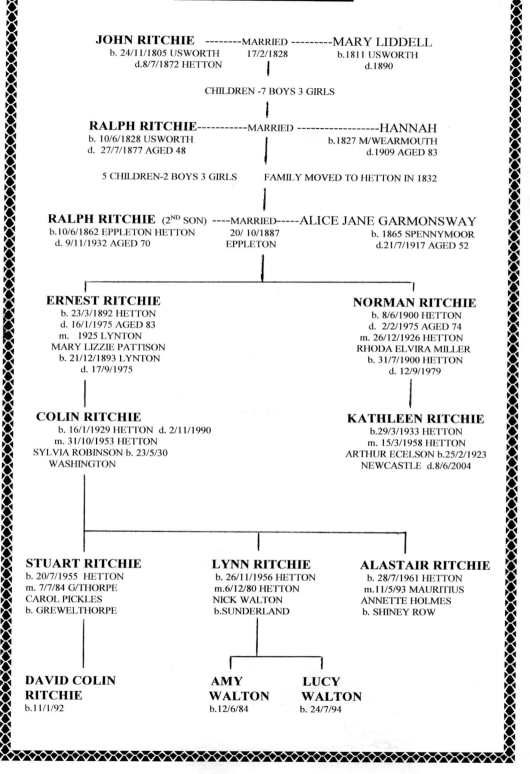

JOHN RITCHIE -------- MARRIED -------- **MARY LIDDELL**
b. 24/11/1805 USWORTH   17/2/1828   b.1811 USWORTH
d.8/7/1872 HETTON   d.1890

CHILDREN -7 BOYS 3 GIRLS

RALPH RITCHIE---------- MARRIED ----------------**HANNAH**
b. 10/6/1828 USWORTH   b.1827 M/WEARMOUTH
d. 27/7/1877 AGED 48   d.1909 AGED 83

5 CHILDREN-2 BOYS 3 GIRLS   FAMILY MOVED TO HETTON IN 1832

RALPH RITCHIE (2ND SON) ----MARRIED-----**ALICE JANE GARMONSWAY**
b.10/6/1862 EPPLETON HETTON   20/ 10/1887   b. 1865 SPENNYMOOR
d. 9/11/1932 AGED 70   EPPLETON   d.21/7/1917 AGED 52

ERNEST RITCHIE
b. 23/3/1892 HETTON
d. 16/1/1975 AGED 83
m. 1925 LYNTON
MARY LIZZIE PATTISON
b. 21/12/1893 LYNTON
d. 17/9/1975

NORMAN RITCHIE
b. 8/6/1900 HETTON
d. 2/2/1975 AGED 74
m. 26/12/1926 HETTON
RHODA ELVIRA MILLER
b. 31/7/1900 HETTON
d. 12/9/1979

COLIN RITCHIE
b. 16/1/1929 HETTON d. 2/11/1990
m. 31/10/1953 HETTON
SYLVIA ROBINSON b. 23/5/30
WASHINGTON

KATHLEEN RITCHIE
b.29/3/1933 HETTON
m. 15/3/1958 HETTON
ARTHUR ECELSON b.25/2/1923
NEWCASTLE d.8/6/2004

STUART RITCHIE
b. 20/7/1955 HETTON
m. 7/7/84 G/THORPE
CAROL PICKLES
b. GREWELTHORPE

LYNN RITCHIE
b. 26/11/1956 HETTON
m.6/12/80 HETTON
NICK WALTON
b.SUNDERLAND

ALASTAIR RITCHIE
b. 28/7/1961 HETTON
m.11/5/93 MAURITIUS
ANNETTE HOLMES
b. SHINEY ROW

**DAVID COLIN
RITCHIE**
b.11/1/92

**AMY
WALTON**
b.12/6/84

**LUCY
WALTON**
b. 24/7/94

The company founder – Ralph Ritchie – is seen above right, while above is his mother Hannah Ritchie. The family shot (right) was taken about 1901 and shows Ralph and his mother. Ralph's wife – Alice Jane - is sat holding their youngest son Norman while their eldest son Ernest is wearing the cap. The other figures are Alice Jane's sister – Lizzie – with her two children Nellie and Tom.

CHAPTER 1

Ralph's Vision

Ralph Ritchie had a dream. Not for him the oppressive purgatory of going down a hole in the ground to dig for coal. Instead he longed for life in the fresh air, the prospect of being his own boss and the dream of making a comfortable living for a family he would love to bring into the world.

But unlike most of us who have simply pondered on what fate – hopefully – could bring, Ralph Ritchie decided to do something about it. So, with every spare penny he could earn, he vowed to turn that dream into reality.

It's not that he wanted to turn his back entirely on the coal industry. Yes, it was the search for coal, which was to drive his father – also called Ralph - into an early grave at the age of 48. True it was the hunger for these black nuggets of fuel, that would also kill his elder brother John at the age of 28 in a tragic pithead accident But in truth, it was the search for coal that had given work to Ralph's forefathers for many years and had created an expertise in engineering which would – eventually – see the Ritchie dream come to fruition.

THE RITCHIE ROOTS

Back in the mists of time, the Ritchie family apparently hark from the Scottish town of Dunfermline. But sensing that heading South of the Border could bring a better life, the early 1700s saw the Ritchie clan ensconced on Tyneside.

This part of the North East of England was to spawn all manner of engineering concerns although it was the similarly dominant coal industry in the area that had originally prompted life long service of many in the Ritchie family. When John Ritchie died (in 1872) the dedication of having spent almost half a century as a engineer at Eppleton Pit was recorded on his gravestone: "As a token of the respect and esteem," which this service had created. Working in a coal mine was certainly hard – and the pay wasn't that good – but one major plus point was in how the pit owners usually provided housing for their workers. When Eppleton Pit was first opened the Ritchie family were to take up residence of No. 1, Pit Cottages. But after Ralph Senior's early death – in 1877 - the family retained the right to live there, as both the two Ritchie sons were to follow their father into Eppleton Pit employ.

However, with the death of his big brother (in 1885) Ralph Ritchie decided to look strongly at his future – and the dreams he held. He had served his time as an engine fitter at Eppleton Pit and found to have natural engineering talents. He was to marry Alice Jane Garmonsway – in 1887 – and persuaded her to follow him with his dream. Moving 23 miles north doesn't seem much to write home about in this day and age but leaving the Hetton-le-Hole area for the intenseness of the Heaton area of Newcastle was in Ralph's time, literally heading for another world.

The big attraction with the move was with the huge increase in pay. The engineering concern of Watsons was a

	No. of Certificate.
	62116.

REGISTRATION OF BUSINESS NAMES ACT, 1916.

CERTIFICATE OF REGISTRATION.

I hereby certify that a Statement

of particulars furnished by *R. Ritchie & Co.*

of *Station Road, Hetton le Hole.*

pursuant to Sections 3 and 4 of the above-mentioned Act was

registered on the 26th day of *April* 1917.

Dated this 26th day of *April* 1917

Bernard Mallet

Registrar of Business Names.

By Sec. 6 of the above Act it is enacted that—
Whenever a change is made or occurs in any of the particulars registered in respect of any firm or person such firm or person shall within fourteen days after such change, or such longer period as the Board of Trade may, on application being made in any particular case, whether before or after the expiration of such fourteen days, allow, furnish by sending by post or delivery to the Registrar in that part of the United Kingdom in which the aforesaid particulars are registered a statement in writing in the prescribed form specifying the nature and date of the change signed, and where necessary verified, in like manner as the statement required on registration.

By Sec. 13 (1)—
If any firm or individual registered under this Act ceases to carry on business, it shall be the duty of the persons who were partners in the firm at the time when it ceased to carry on business, or of the individual or if he is dead his personal representative, within three months after the business has ceased to be carried on, to send by post or deliver to the registrar notice in the prescribed form that the firm or individual has ceased to carry on business, and if any person whose duty it is to give such notice fails to do so within such time as aforesaid, he shall be liable on summary conviction to a fine not exceeding twenty pounds.

Forms of notification of change or cessation may be obtained from the REGISTRAR OF BUSINESS NAMES, 39, RUSSELL SQUARE, LONDON, W.C.

(X 407) Wt. 54354/831. 2/17. 300m. Drayton Mill. (903)

hugely respected company on Tyneside and they were to pay a huge sum (when compared to the pit owners) for the engineering talents of Ralph Ritchie.

If you want to see those talents on show, then head for the dramatically set Cragside House, just outside Rothbury in Northumberland. Although now part of the National Trust, in the 1880s, the house was owned by Lord Armstrong and was fitted with hot & cold running water, central heating, fire alarms & telephones and was apparently the first house in the world to be lit by electricity. And, apparently, Ralph Ritchie was one of the chosen engineers to work on this revolutionary project.

It is imagined that Ralph would enjoy a good bonus or two with this work and any extra cash was earmarked to fulfil his dream. The Watson management wouldn't know what Ralph had in mind but as time passed (and his savings grew) Ralph made regular trips back to his hometown of Hetton, to buy up sections of land. In total, six acres of open pasture were bought from the Bowes Lyon family over a period of 10 years and by 1898, the Ritchie dream was set to become reality.

TRIUMPH GARAGE

The move back to Hetton couldn't have come any later for Ralph's wife Alice Jane. The oppressive smoggy air surrounding their rented house on Tyneside had played havoc with her general well being, but Ralph's dream had kept them both going to stay long enough to build up the capital they needed.

As well as the land, the money was to be invested in the building of the later named Triumph Garage (it was certainly a triumph to achieve your dream). This is still the hub of the Ritchie organisation and it's now used as an office & been extended to accommodate workshops and purpose built warehousing. But back in 1898, Ralph created a hardware shop – at the front - and an entirely separate engineering area plus a blacksmith's shop, out back.

Selling all manner of wares (glass & chinaware was apparently imported by the East India Company) to the locals of Hetton, the Ritchie shop was also to supply tea. It arrived in town – in tea chests - by train (Hetton station was only about 200 yards up the road) and was collected by one of the three Ritchie horses and carts. The imported tea was naturally sold off in smaller amounts, but the main earner for the growing Ritchie organisation was in the founder's engineering abilities. There may have been other cycle repairers in town but no one could make mangle rollers & wheels – for domestic clothes washing – the way Ritchies could do. As fine turners of the best quality wood, Ritchies also made wooden rolling pins and with carefully placed advertising, the varied Ritchie services were being used by one and all.

As extra employment for their horses and carts, Ralph worked for the local Hetton Council. The job wasn't particularly nice to talk about (it was worse to do) but cleaning the outside toilets of the Hetton houses was a regular earner for Ritchies. When flushing toilets were still in their infancy, the standard loo was simply a seat above a pile of ash in a shed at the bottom of the yard. The bodily waste was removed – through an outer hatch of the back-to-back, terrace houses - by the Ritchie team and fresh ash put in its place. It was an awful job, but someone had to do it. And compared to what happened in 1914, you could say it was a positive – and peaceful - pleasure.

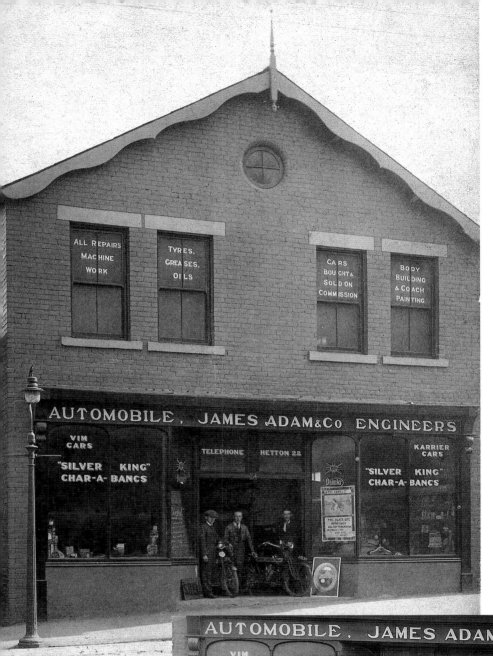

During the 1914-18 World War I, the Ritchie front showroom was taken over by James Adams & Co. The 17-year-old Norman Ritchie is believed to be the figure in the centre of the lower shot. All three men of the Ritchie family – Ralph, Ernest and Norman – were to become directors in the Adams business before branching out into charabanc operations by themselves.

CHAPTER 2

E & N –
Ernest and Norman

Ralph and Alice Ritchie were to have two sons. Ernest was born in 1892 while younger brother Norman was born in 1900. The eight years difference was more noticeable when they were young, because as time passed, the brothers were to combine their business – and engineering – talents to forge a strong marker of the Ritchie presence in the North East of England.

In 1914, however, the main concern of the family was simply about keeping the business going. As part of the World War I effort, Ralph Ritchie was seconded to work back in the engineering and munitions factories in Newcastle. He knew his wife Alice Jane couldn't take the move back to Tyneside so while she stayed on at their home in Hetton, every Monday morning, Ralph left on foot and walked the 20 miles or so, to work in Newcastle. Staying all week in accommodation, he would walk home again for his weekend off.

The hard work ethic was obviously shared by all of the Ritchie family as Alice Jane had long been running a small confectionery and bakery shop from the front room of their terrace house at 77, The Avenue. However, the outbreak of war forced the Ritchie family to close their larger hardware shop on Station Road. This shop was then converted into a showroom and for the duration of the war was leased by James Adams, a car dealer and charabanc operator.

The two Ritchie brothers were to keep the engineering side of affairs ticking over. And of course, there was always work for the toilet emptying Ritchie horses and carts. However, again as part of the war effort, both Ernest and Norman were seconded to work on Wakefield's Great Eppleton farm and were to learn the craft of being able to plough a straight furrow using horses. This proved to be a very enjoyable experience for both the young Ritchies and created such an impression, that being around farmers – and the farming way of life – always remained of great interest to them.

Norman was also expected to help out with the core Ritchie activity of roller making. These just didn't go into washing mangles because when Rhoda Elvira Miller walked into the shop, she was after a roller for a window blind.

Rhoda had worked as the maid for the Robinson family in Hetton ever since she'd left school at the age of 14 (being paid a modest 2/6d - 12.5p - per week) but was soon smitten with young Norman. It made a huge impression on Rhoda that Norman would saddle up one of the Ritchie horses and ride up town to see her. So it's perhaps not surprising that after a long courtship, Rhoda and Norman would marry – in 1926. Elder brother Ernest had married Mary Lizzie Patterson, the previous year – 1925. She had never liked her middle name and always said children should simply be given a number until they were old enough to pick a name for themselves. Mary Lizzie's father was a Colliery Manager at Linton, near Ashington in Northumberland although Mary had travelled down to London in 1914 and took up nursing as part of the war effort. It was only a chance holiday in Hetton (with her friend Alice Bolton) that was to bring Mary and Ernest together.

CHARABANCS

The end of the First World War was to herald major changes for the Ritchie business. Ralph's wife - Alice Jane - died (at the age of 54) in 1917 and her front room shop in the Avenue was closed. And while, the Ritchies took back their show room from James Adams, there was no inclination to return to the hardware business.

Turning rollers and mangle wheels was still a natural activity for Ralph Ritchie, who had no inclination to try out these new fangled things called motor vehicles. However, his two sons quickly identified that the mechanised load carrier was going to be a big earner.

First freight for the internal combustion powered Ritchie vehicles was actually to be passengers. Ernest & Norman were to take over the two Karrier charabancs operated (under the name of The Silver King) by James Adams but soon took delivery of an ex Royal Flying Corps Crossley ambulance chassis. Sent to what later became the Eastern Coach Works at Bracebridge Heath, Lincoln, this was equipped with a smart body, which could seat 14 passengers. While some charabancs were made so their seat-equipped bodies could be interchanged (so they could then carry freight) the Ritchie ones were all fixed. Norman was to become the regular driver of this new Crossley and as a trading name, J 9135 ran under the banner of Triumph.

BLACKPOOL BOUND

The Ritchie business had all been started because of Ralph Ritchie's dream and in

essence, the Ritchie charabancs fulfilled many other people's dreams. In the 21st century a trip to Blackpool may not seem anything exotic but back in the early 1920s, it was the dream of many North Easterners just to see that far off Golden Mile and get to the top of the 519' high Blackpool Tower. The Ritchie charabancs went all over the North on private hire trips although the run to Blackpool was a good earner as 30/- per head - £1.50 – was charged for the 260 mile round trip. Running over the top of the Pennines via Piercebridge, Brough and Kendal was exceptionally hard going for Norman and the Crossley, but if extra passengers had to be carried, then these were accommodated in the Ford Model T car PT 1017, which followed behind. Such a trip took its toll on the little Ford and to ensure it could get back to Hetton, Ernest & Norman would often strip the Ford engine on the sea front at Blackpool and give it a quick de-coke and overhaul.

The two brothers soon built up a great working knowledge of the Northern road network and it's just as well as the lighting fitted to motors of the early '20s was fairly modest. The oil lamps were also prone to being blown out – by the buffeting wind – and while the brothers could easily drive without lights, they often found it difficult to dodge the Kirby Stephen Policeman, if he was in a bad mood or wanting to get some cases in his book.

When you carry so many people over so much distance all sorts can happen. On one trip to Saltburn, Norman invited Rhoda as he had a spare seat but when they reached Ormesby, Rhoda was suffering from excruciating stomach pains. Spotting a small cottage, Norman asked the householder if Rhoda could rest there but as soon as he delivered the party to Saltburn, he returned to collect her and quickly took her home. The urgency was shown to be worthwhile, as Rhoda had suffered an abscess on her appendix and required hospitalisation for 14 weeks.

On a different trip, Norman had plenty of

1922.   Bookings

June 5th — Reeth   booked   by Mr. W. F. Holmes. 10/- a head
leave at 8-30 A.M.   via Piercebridge & Darlington

June 10th — Whitley Bay. (Hetton P. M.) (5/- a head) via N/c. 9 A.M.
C. E. Boy's   1/6 a head.

June 17th — Easington Colly. (Football match) 2 loads.

" 21st — N/c   Races.   5/- a head.

22nd — N/c   do   5/-   a   head.

24th — Dawdon   to Gilsland. (Mr. Harrison) 12/6 a head.

July 1st — West Stanley. (Football match) 3/6 a head.

" 3rd — Houghton to Whitley 4/6 a head. (leave 9-15.

" 12th — Alnwick. (County Show) 10/- a head. leave 8 A.M.

July 22nd — Horden to Blackpool (Mrs Nobel 23 First St
Horden) @ 30/- a head. return monday July 31. Tuesday Aug 1st

August 2nd — Wolsingham (County Show) 5/- a head. leave 9 A.M.

" 3rd — Houghton to Whitley Bay 5/6 a head via N/c

5th — Hetton to Whitley

6th — Hetton to Lake District 30/- a head.
return Aug 7th via Alston & Hexham.

12th — Horden to Whitley Bay 6/- a head.
booked by Mrs Nobel 23 1st Street Horden

14th — Hetton to Whitley Bay   Lyons aged miners. 4/6 a head

19th — Hetton to Rothbury & Alnwick via Newcastle. 11/- a head.
booked by Mr. Milburn. Caroline St. Hetton.

over

15

Income.

DATE	HIRERS	ROUTE	MILES	PRICE	GROSS PROFIT.
July 12th	Northumberland County Show	ALNWICK VIA N/C.	100	10/- A. HEAD. 14 passengers	£7-0-0
July 22nd	Mrs Nobel 23 First Street Horden.	Blackpool	260	30/- A. HEAD. 14 passengers.	£21-0-0
July 26th	Party.	Blackpool To Southport	75	6/6 A. HEAD 12 passengers.	£3-18-0
July 30th	Party.	Blackpool To St Annes.	10	1/6 a head. 13. passengers.	£0-19-6
Aug 2nd	County Show.	Wolsingham via Crook.		5/- a head 14 passengers.	£3-10-0
Aug 3rd	Mrs Howe. Sunderland St Houghton.	Whitley Bay via n/c.	50	5/- a head 14 passengers.	£3-10-0
Aug 5th	Miss Miller Lyons Street Hetton Downs.	Whitley Bay via h/c	50	4/6 a head 14 passengers	£3-3-0
Aug 6th	W. F. Holmes	Lake District via Penrith return via Alston	228.	30/- a head 13 passengers.	£19-10-0 ———— Cap½ Gross Profit.
Aug 12th	Mrs Nobel Horden	Whitley Bay via h/c	67.	5/- a head 14 passengers	£3-10-0

empty seats but no one wanted to fill them.

Following a tragic accident at the picturesque Aysgarth Falls (in the Yorkshire Dales) a young boy was drowned and Ritchies were asked to take the boy's father and an empty coffin, to collect the boy's body. Befitting the occasion, the weather for the trip was vile and Norman could long recall that almost never ending journey back to Hetton with the father in tears as the coffin swayed around behind them.

THE TRUSTY T

The modest Ford Model T was to start many in the road haulage business and E&N Ritchie adopted these converted cars as their first load carriers. However, It wasn't long before a heavier duty Ford (30 cwt) and a spoke wheeled 1 ton Morris were in service. While the charabancs were great earners, the private hire trips could only be done when folk weren't at work. So while the two brothers did these runs on a weekend and the summer evenings, they spent their days on general haulage.

There was no requirement for any licences (or limits on drivers hours) until 1933 although the practical operation of some transport in the 1920s saw the rail network carry the cargo over the longer distance and then the local small road haulier – like Ritchies – collect this from the railway station and deliver it to the customer.

Such an early link was forged with R Silcock & Sons, the cattle food manufacturer of Liverpool. They used Ritchies for collecting the bagged feed from the railway yards of both Hetton and Norton (near Stockton-on-Tees) for distribution around the local farms. As this trade built up, Ritchies stored the feed first in the garage and then built a purpose built 'Cake' store, as it was called. Incorporating two loading bays – at the height of a vehicle's platform – it was highly advanced for the era – and for such a small company. This proved good, regular work for Ritchies although there was

a major panic when three railway vans came loaded with Silcock's feed and the London and North Eastern Railway (LNER) management demanded that Ritchies clear the vans immediately.

Because the Ritchie boys soon established a reputation of being hard workers, regular work came their way. This varied in the extreme as a check of the brother's time sheets of the mid '20s revealed a huge variety of work. Delivering groceries for the large North East grocery concern of Broughs (with up to 110 different house calls per round) gave regular contract work for two wagons, while a horse and cart was also used for the deliveries from Brough's Hetton branch. This particular horse was called Taffy and is recalled as being the fastest Grey in the area, but more of him later.

Fresh fish was a regular collection from the fish quay at Hartlepool and is recalled as being the cargo that Norman was carrying when he was stopped by a picket line during the General Strike of 1926: 'Do you want your fish suppers tonight,' Norman apparently asked as to whether they would let him proceed. And when the reply came that of course they did, then Norman – and the fish - was allowed to pass through the line.

Attending the cattle marts at Newcastle and Fencehouses produced deliveries to the butchers in Seaham, Hetton and Houghton. The vehicles would require cleaning – and fresh straw – between loads and the smell of Jeyes Fluid was to become a recognised aroma for all involved, for many a year. The brothers love of the farming life also meant Ritchies were involved in taking the best of beasts to the annual Durham County Show. Ernest recalled that a small mint sweet was the best thing to feed sheep if you wanted to keep them happy. Naturally the Ritchie vehicles were adapted to carry cows, sheep and pigs although it was modifications of an entirely different kind to the fleet that was soon being fitted.

It was a memorable day when the Ritchie family launched themselves into the motorised age with this ex Royal Flying Corps Crossley ambulance chassis. Converted for passenger transport, it's also been converted to have electric headlights although the side lamps are still illuminated by oil. Fitting – or removing - the concertina style of roof would probably take two men about five minutes as each of the locating stanchions had wing nuts to hold them in place. Side screens were carried and could also be fitted if the weather was particularly bad. Seen in the background is the old Hetton Lyons Colliery railway line built by Robert Stephenson (son of George Stephenson, the famous builder of the 'Rocket' rail locomotive).

Norman Ritchie's first driving licence was issued on 18th April 1921 (at a cost of 5/- or 25p) and he was to become the Crossley's regular driver. It was part of the joy of riding with Norman to feel the wind in your hair although Mrs Willis – first row centre – would have ensured her large hat was firmly tied down. About to leave on a run, the Crossley is pictured outside Martins Bank, in Hetton town centre.

(Top) It was perhaps fitting that William Holmes (a relative of the Ritchie family) made the first ever booking for the Ritchie charabanc on 5th June 1922. The party from the local Chapel left Hetton at 8.30am and travelled via Piercebridge (and returned via Darlington) to the beautiful North Yorkshire village of Reeth. It's not sure if this was a record of that event although the backdrop is believed to be the popular village green at Reeth. It's recorded that 14 gallons of petrol were used that day costing Ritchies £1-15s (which in modern terms equates to 12.5p per gallon).

Due to the large amount of work he did there, Ralph Ritchie was to have a close affinity with the huge Cragside Estate in Northumberland. The National Trust now owns the house and grounds but on 19th August 1922, Ralph's son Norman took a detour from a trip to Rothbury just for this photo call.

(Left) A 21st century trip from Hetton to Blackpool could be undertaken as a short day run but back in July 1922, it was a week long adventure for driver Norman Ritchie and his party of 14 passengers who paid £1.10s each for the 260 mile return journey. Norman is pictured at Blackpool and while he too stayed for the week, he earned more revenue with day trips to Southport (6/6d per head) and to Lytham St Anne's – for 1/6d each.

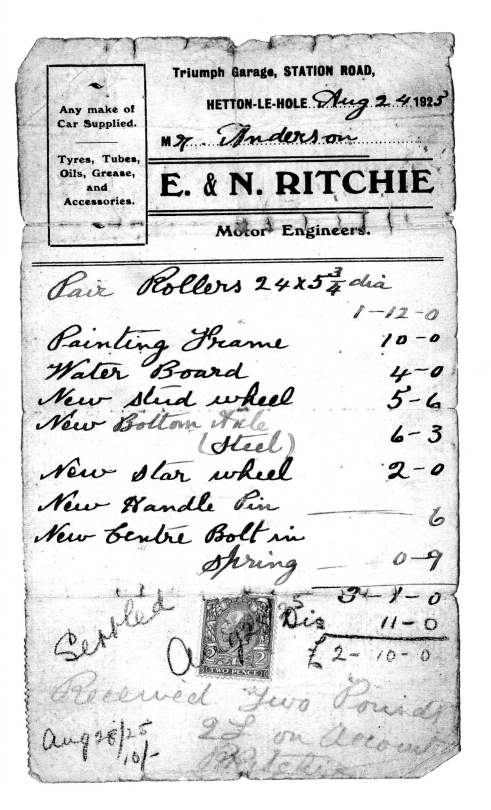

Triumph Garage, STATION ROAD,

HETTON-LE-HOLE *Aug 24 1925*

M⟨r⟩ *Anderson*

E. & N. RITCHIE

Motor Engineers.

Any make of Car Supplied.

Tyres, Tubes, Oils, Grease, and Accessories.

Pair Rollers 24 x 5¾ dia	1 – 12 – 0
Painting Frame	10 – 0
Water Board	4 – 0
New Stud wheel	5 – 6
New Bottom Axle (Steel)	6 – 3
New Star wheel	2 – 0
New Handle Pin	6
New Centre Bolt in Spring	0 – 9
	3 – 1 – 0
Dis	11 – 0
	£ 2 – 10 – 0

Settled

Received Two Pounds
Aug 28/25   2 £ on Account
/0/-

E. & N.

WORK SHEET

Day	Wagon No.	
Monday	2	Har
Tuesday	2	Doc / Rain
Wednesday	2	Fis Har / Lo Geo.
Thursday	2	Har
Friday	2	Har
Saturday	2	Ha / Thurs / F.

20

ITCHIE, Triumph Garage, Station Road, HETTON-LE-HOLE.

Week Ending _Dec 24th_ 192 7.   Name _ER_

tion.	Time From	To	Petrol Gals.	Oil Pints	Approx. Miles	Approx. Weight	Description of Goods Carried.
pool	9-30	4-30	5	1	44	15 cwts	Fish.
							Signed.
(Hetton)	11-15	12.				Tons 5	3/4 hour 1 load blocks. ⎫ ✓
	1	4	—	—	12		3 hours. 4 " " " ⎭
Colly					marks	Toucet 1-5	Hall (Coals) Paid .
						6-5	_Signed._
pool.	9-30	4	3	1	38	10 cwts	Fish .
ide.					9		Vale
					47		Leanside N.R. Magneto. _Signed._
pool	9-30	4-30	2	—	44.	15 cwts	Fish
							Signed.
bool.	9-30	4-30	2	1	40	18 cwts	Fish
							Signed.
pool	9-15	1-30	2	—	40	4 cwts	Fish
House	3-15	8	—	—	24.		Stephenson's _Signed._

The Ritchie account (left) gives some indication of the number of parts the business could both manufacture and supply when it came to mangles and rollers. One question, which no one in the current Ritchie family could answer, was to why the big discount. The 1927 work sheet (above) tells of a typical week of Ernest Ritchie with fish being still a staple traffic. And of course there was no early finish for Ernie – even on Christmas Eve – if there was work to be done.

During the mid 1920s, the brothers took time out to be married. While Ernest's marriage to Mary Lizzie Pattison (left) in 1925 seemed a grand affair, no photographs were apparently taken when Norman and Rhoda Elvira Miller married on Boxing Day in 1926. Both are pictured (below) in their younger days although both these marriages were to last almost 50 years.

CHAPTER 3

Hetton Sand & Gravel

The 1930s was a traumatic time for the entire country. As an apparent knock on to the General Strike of 1926, the '30s seemed a never-ending period of depression. Stagnation of business meant survival was paramount amongst most people's objectives. Norman Ritchie had to use all his guile as a salesman to drum up trade for the modest Ritchie concern as competition was rife. The company ledgers of the time are full of various quotations – from a variety of other people – as this knowledge was highly important if your quote – for the same or similar work - was to be accepted. And picking up information in that vein meant a certain amount of subterfuge – or downright spying – had to be undertaken.

However, when the Government decided to encourage the building of Council houses, such work proved to be a godsend to companies like E & N Ritchie. Yes, while the North East of England may have been well known for its rich deposits of coal, even closer to the surface where rich swathes of sand and gravel. Once the relevant licensing agreements regarding extraction were signed, Ernest and Norman established Hetton Sand & Gravel Co Ltd as buying, selling, extracting and transporting agents for this class of material.

The new business (formalised on 28th September 1934) saw the two brothers with equal holdings of 500 shares each. The new company signalled a change in direction away from the ways of their father and even the well-loved charabancs were pensioned off. Other larger concerns were structuring regular bus services and even the rail network was creating more services – at a more competitive rate – for away day travellers. The Ritchie capacity of 14 passengers in their Crossley was no longer viable.

Ralph Ritchie had remained involved in the business right up to his death on 9th November 1932 at the age of 70. Even when he was too infirm to walk the short distance to the garage, he arranged to be transported there by being carried in a wheelbarrow. His beloved lathes were to lie quiet after his death as apart from the odd repair or two, the trade of dealing in mangles and rollers was passed to other concerns.

To handle the bulk sand & gravel material, the two brothers were to obviously invest in four wheeled tippers. However, Tom Soulsby recalls that buying anything at all prompted the most protracted of discussions and heart searching. Tom (who was related to E&N through marriage) joined the company in 1935 aged 16 as an Office Clerk. He noted it was a Ritchie trait to always consider prudence as their mainstay as Ralph Ritchie had always said to his two sons they should only buy something if they had the money to pay for it.

The gift of hindsight suggests the Ritchies could have been millionaires if they'd invested in a neighbouring venture (into larger deposits of sand & gravel extraction). However, risking the loan of £2,000 was

Ritchie's big Vulcan 2.5 tonner PT 8672 is seen with driver Hughie Race. Fitted with solid rubber tyres, it was bought new on 21st June 1932. The Ritchie records say that it cost them £500 but for some reason it was apparently sold to Horden Collieries Ltd in July 1933 for only £47-10s.

given short shrift by Ernest – and not even discussed with Norman. Instead, keeping within their means saw the business enjoy a very gradual growth as a pillar of the local community.

A HORSE NAMED TAFFY

The two brothers love of both the farming way of life and animals in general were to have several long-term influences on the company. About 1931 they sectioned off part of the yard and began breeding pigs - and even imported a special pig man from Yorkshire to look after them. The sausage meat produced from these pigs is recalled as being particularly delicious but the project had mixed financial success. And it came to a premature end in 1938 when a severe dose of swine fever prompted the whole herd to be put down.

Although the mechanised load carrier

was the way forward, the brothers retained the use of horses until well into the 1940s. That choice was probably taken because of the long service given by Taffy.

All animals are characters in their own right but Taffy was something special. It was particularly strong and fast across the ground, as it couldn't seem to walk slowly on its huge feet. Being used for the distribution of groceries around the Hetton area was ideal work for one man and his horse and Taffy apparently knew his round like clockwork. Tale is told of how the driver – after his work was done – would often stop off at a local hostelry and leave his horse & cart outside. Taffy would soon tire of just hanging around so he would simply walk back to the yard and could even turn the tap on to pour himself a drink. When out to grass, if it started to rain he had this habit of walking over to the stables and even if the door wasn't fully open, he'd poke

Ritchies were hauling sand & gravel in bulk during the late 1920s but the business was to be transformed when Ernest & Norman formed Hetton Sand & Gravel Ltd. While materials were to be extracted – under licence – in all parts of the North East of England, the quarry at Fallowfield proved to be the family's best local source. Jackie Ferguson, the driver of this Bedford 2 tonner – is seen on the left. He shares the picture with Jackie Teasdale, who went on to do 25 years service at Ritchies, generally in quarry related matters. Ritchies meticulous records reveal that when this 1931 Bedford (unladen weight 1 ton 17 cwt.) was filled 3-4" from the top of its body, it carried 3 tons of gravel. BR 8878 (chassis no. 103328) was traded in by Ritchies in July 1934, when £90 was given by the Buist dealership in part exchange for a two ton Morris UP 9518. Ritchies paid a total of £263 for the new Morris although £6 of that were its delivery charges. No complaints from the Ritchies as this Morris stayed in service until scrapped in 1951 and there were no complaints that the Bedford went because this was a flat (and had to be unloaded using a shovel) while the new Morris had mechanical means to tip off its load.

his head inside just to keep the top part of his body dry. In many respects he was quite human and always gave a tremendous workload to the Ritchie business. He was also something of a pest as if stabled together with the other horse Dick, he'd think nothing of taking a nip or two out of Dick's flesh. The next time, Dick would feel any sort of touch, he'd lash out – even if the touch was from guys like George Kirkbride, who had come into the stable to feed him.

WAGON LADS

George had started at Ritchies at the age of 14 in 1929 as a wagon lad although as Norman Ritchie was his Uncle, he'd tended to haunt the Ritchie garage as a boy: 'There was a small seat in the charabanc to the offside of the driver,' George recalls, 'and Uncle Norman would let me sit there. I was also allowed to blow the klaxon horn and he even told me to stick my arm out if we were turning right. I loved being involved.'

Working at Ritchies was something of a mixed blessing as Ernest and Norman had different ways of talking to him: 'If Ernest had suffered a bad week,' says George, 'he could often fire me on a Friday – although Norman would say I should just start again on the Monday. Although it was their father – Ralph – who always assured me it was still his business and I worked for him, just as his two sons did.'

Being a wagon lad meant you obviously helped with deliveries & collections although first job for George – and the other lads - was to crank start the motors on a morning: 'In the winter we'd have to take the spark plugs out of the engine and warm them up on the stove just so they'd fire up better,' he says of a job that was rarely easy. Of all the runs George did, the ride into Newcastle with Norman and the big Vulcan 3 tonner was the most memorable: 'It was originally fitted with solid wheels all round and it would shake you to bits,' he says. 'But once we reached Low Fell, Norman would drop the wheels into the tram lines and he could take his hands off the steering wheel as the tracks did the steering. It was nice and smooth then but it was a bit of a panic to get out of the tracks if we saw a tram coming towards us.' Worst job was if they'd gone to North Shields or Hartlepool for a load of fresh fish: 'It was the job of the wagon lad to wash the motor off after we'd unloaded and the fish was awfully smelly.'

Being versatile was all part & parcel of a life at Ritchies. You had to be able to handle the horses but also strong enough to handle 1 cwt bags of flour and even sacks of sugar that weighed in at 1.5 cwts: 'The little sack barrow was your best friend in those days,' recalls George. And once the Hetton Sand & Gravel work picked up, you also had to be strong enough to wind the screw tipper bodies up.

As soon as he was old enough, George moved onto driving: 'I used to watch Norman and just copied what he did,' he says. 'My driving test was when he took me up to the Golf Course road with the small Morris and once I showed I could drive alright then that was it.'

George was to have some happy days either with his little Guy or a second hand Vulcan that was bought: 'I wasn't too struck on the cattle work,' he says, 'but every Friday, I enjoyed heading out of Newcastle Market and up the valley towards Chopwell on deliveries. It was great being your own boss.'

Not much fun on the day he was coming up Leamside and his two rear nearside wheels came off: 'I think the rear hubs had got changed round when the vehicle was being serviced so the wheel nuts just unscrewed themselves.'

No panic for George who simply packed the axle up and put the wheels back on. He did of course have to unload his beasts into a nearby field before doing this although getting them back onto the wagon was more of a problem.

THE ELITE

In his first 11-year stint at Ritchies, George reckoned he was never amongst the elite. The company was split into different activities during the '30s with the sand & gravel operation being very local. George would run into Newcastle and get around Durham County on local work, his instructions for the day normally being written on a small piece of paper, which was clamped into the garage vice for his early morning attention. However, the elite team at Ritchies were Ralph Bleanch, Hughie Race and Matty Hall, the long distance guys.

Long distance for Ritchies were the regular trips down to the British Oil & Cake Mills at Hull and being so far, it always merited a night out at the regular stop of Norman Johnson's bed & breakfast at Thirsk in North Yorkshire.

Back at HQ, the Ritchies garage did servicing and repairs of other vehicles (they were agents for Lea Francis cars and also became a dealership for Morris Cars until that agreement lapsed in 1972). The company also sold Pyramid Petrol (at 1/2d – 6p – per gallon) and a hand-operated pump dispensed this. Several full rotations of the pump's winding handle would dispense one full gallon but prior to the next gallon's discharge, the handle had to be fully rotated back to its starting position.

Although there wasn't a huge amount of petrol sold at that time (except when the travelling Fair came to town and the showmen needed fuel for their generators) the Ritchie yard was a hive of industry once the sand & gravel plant was erected, behind the garage. At first the company had used a mobile type of grader hauled by a Crossley tractor (PT 5270) that did the rounds of various sand & gravel pits. But once Ernest

26

and Norman had made the decision to have the Leicester concern of Goodwin Barsby & Co Ltd install their overhead rotary grader, the system was more established.

Washing the sand and also grading the gravel (into two specific sizes) was made easy because the Ritchie brothers dammed the adjacent beck and used the water from there to clean the material. To Norman's daughter – Kathleen – the plant is recalled as looking like a Heath Robinson affair but the fact it lasted almost 40 years lays testament to its simple efficiency.

Kathleen recalls she was never allowed to go anywhere near the garage: 'I suppose it was because I was a girl,' she says, 'and young girls didn't really play around lorries and the like.' The one day a friend and her were tempted to stray down to the garage almost ended in disaster: 'The area where the silt was filtered off into looked like a beach and a friend suggested we play there. But when I walked in, it was like walking on quicksand and I just sank. Fortunately my father had a premonition something was wrong and when he spotted I wasn't playing outside, he ran down to the garage and rescued me.'

Being a boy, there was no such restraint from playing in the yard on Ernest's son Colin. It's not surprising that Colin would eventually take over the reins of the E&N Ritchie business (more than 30 years later) although before then, the family – and the entire country – had another World War to contend with.

Ritchies were to have a variety of success from their Vulcans and WM 9430 was considered to be their fleet flagship when it was registered new on 6th September 1933. With chassis number 50 RF 2470, the 2.5 tonner was operated both as a tipper and a cattle wagon. With a purchase price of £526-6s – and an unladen weight of 2 tons 19cwt – it was simply a matter of removing / replacing the sides as and when cattle were to be carried. When it was scrapped in August 1939, the engine and gearbox were kept for spares.

Bought new on 3rd May 1930, this Guy – UP 4310 – was nominally rated as having a 30cwt capacity. With chassis number O.N.9624, its first major overhaul was done after 50,000 miles. This saw the cylinders re-bored, specialised pistons fitted and attention given to the big end bearings and the rocker joints. Including work on the gearbox, the cost of the parts was given as just over £14. In July 1937, the Guy was transferred to the Hetton Sand & Gravel fleet.

WM 9430 is seen again in working guise. Ritchies were to buy their fourth Vulcan (another 2.5 ton tipper) second hand in 1937 from the Newcastle based FW Cawthorn for the sum of £110-10s. Chassis no. 2 HF 1008 also had detachable sides and was new on 1st June 1935.

Ritchies were to take a solid wheeled Halley four wheeled flat from Hetton Co-op (as part of the deal when they took over their transport) and while no photographs are available of that vehicle, Halley expert Jim Wilkinson drew this from his vast memory.

THE ROAD HAULAGE ASSOCIATION
(Limited by Guarantee.)

This is to Certify that

E. & N. RITCHIE

OF   Triumph Garage, Station Road, Hetton-le-Hole,
Co.Durham.

WAS THIS DAY ELECTED A MEMBER OF

THE ROAD HAULAGE ASSOCIATION

Given under the Seal of the Association

this   29th   *day of*   November   1933.

⎱ *Members
of the
Council.*

Secretary.

REGISTERED No.   2411.

*In the event of non-payment of a member's subscription within three months after the same becomes due,
Membership of the Association will be forfeited.*

THE ROAD HAULAGE ASSOCIATION.
(Limited by Guarantee.)

No. 3769

Area North

11 November 1933.

Received from Mrs E & N. Ritchie
Triumph Garage Station Road. Hetton le Hole Durham

the sum of   four   pounds   ten   shillings   —   pence

for the undermentioned items.

DETAILS:	£	s.	d.
ENTRANCE FEE	1	1	:
ANNUAL SUBSCRIPTION	1	1	:
PERSONAL SUBSCRIPTION			
VEHICLE SUBSCRIPTION	2	8	:
GOODS SUPPLIED			
		:	
		:	
£	4	10	:

For and on behalf of the R.H.A.

Secretary.

In 1933 the Road Haulage Association accepted E&N Ritchie's application for membership. As an Association run by Haulage Contractors on democratic lines for Haulage contractors, in an accompanying pamphlet it warned that: 'Our competitors, the Railways, are a well organised machine so far as propaganda is concerned. The RHA by banding hauliers together is now able to state the road transport case with equal authority. You should pull your weight.' Offering a free legal defence scheme – 'which you cannot afford to ignore' – it also said that it could do something to improve rates: 'If every haulier would support it but success depends on the power of its membership.'

29

OU 1933 (handwritten, top left margin)

MORRIS MOTORS LIMITED
COWLEY, OXFORD

MORRIS
(Regd. Trade Mark)

SPARE PARTS AGREEMENT

Season 1934
(1st September, 1933, to 31st August, 1934)

Agreement made the ___28th___ day of ___April___ 193_4_,

between MORRIS MOTORS LIMITED, of COWLEY, IN THE COUNTY OF OXFORD (hereinafter called the Company) of the one part and Messrs. _E & N. RITCHIE_

of (address) _TRIUMPH GARAGE. STATION ROAD. HETTON-LE-HOLE._

(hereinafter called the Trader) of the other part, through the Company's Authorised and

Appointed Distributor / Dealer Messrs. _TURVEY & CO LTD._

of (town) _SUNDERLAND._

Whereby it is Agreed as follows:—

Definition.
1. The term Morris Spare Parts in this agreement shall be deemed to mean the genuine spare or replacement parts that are manufactured and/or supplied by the Company.

Supply of Parts.
2. The Trader agrees to purchase Morris Spare Parts from the Company's Authorised Distributors or Dealers, delivered free at the Distributors' or Dealers' premises, or from the Company, F.O.R. Factory, at the Company's Price List for Spare Parts current from time to time, less a discount of 15%.

Consequent upon signing this agreement and the undertaking contained in Clause 4 the Trader shall however purchase certain Spare Parts particularly specified in the Company's Spare Parts List from the Company's Authorised Distributors or Dealers, delivered free at the Distributors' or Dealers' premises, or from the Company, F.O.R. Factory, less a discount of 25%.

Selling Prices.
3. The Trader agrees to supply Morris Spare Parts at the Company's Spare Parts List Prices strictly net.

Counterfeit Parts.
4. The Trader undertakes not to purchase or supply or cause to be purchased or supplied any Parts for Morris Cars, Vans and Chassis other than those of the Company's manufacture and supplied (proprietary parts excepted) by the Company.

5. The Trader undertakes prominently to display in his premises a plaque provided by the Company, bearing the words "We supply only genuine Morris Spare Parts."

This Agreement shall terminate on the thirty-first day of August, 1934, in any event.

X/We, _E & N. Ritchie_ ___having carefully read all the Clauses in this Agreement do undertake to abide by the same._ PER PRO E. & N. RITCHIE.

Ernest Ritchie

(Trader).

Signature of Company's Authorised and Appointed Distributor ~~or Dealer~~

Turvey & Co Ltd Humbert Director

Address _Holmeside Sunderland_

Signature for the Company { Per pro. MORRIS MOTORS LTD.

W. M. W. Thomas.

General Sales Manager.

M.O.P. 21761

30

DURHAM DISTRICT (COAL MINES) SCHEME, 1930

TELEGRAPHIC ADDRESS: "QUOTA, NEWCASTLE ON TYNE."

TELEPHONE: 28494.

WM. COUPLAND,
SECRETARY TO THE EXECUTIVE BOARD

Private and Confidential.

31, Mosley Street,
Newcastle upon Tyne, 1.

2nd October, 1936.

Dear Sir(s),

Register of Distributors.

Under the revised Durham District (Coal Mines) Scheme the Sales Control Committee are unable to issue permits for the supply of coal to or through the agency of any Distributor whose name is not upon a Register which will be kept by the Executive Board.

An application has been made for your name to be included upon such Register, and in case that is your desire, I am enclosing agreement for completion and return.

If you are not a distributor of coal, or do not desire to have your name entered on the Register, will you kindly advise me.

Yours faithfully,

Wm Coupland

Secretary.

Agreement
retd Oct 15/36.

Letter sent Oct 3/36.
from H.S.N.G. Co

see file.

'PHONE: JESMOND 1041.　　　　　　　　　　　　10205

　# MINORIES GARAGE.　

PROPRIETORS: R. RANKIN & SONS, LTD.

. JESMOND ROAD,
NEWCASTLE-UPON-TYNE.

AUTOMOBILE ENGINEERS AND MOTOR AGENTS.

Messrs. E. & N. Ritchie.　　　　　2n.d April　　　1937.
　　Triumph Garage,
　　　Station Road,
　　　HETTON.LE.HOLE.

	£	s	d
TO:			
One - N.5. COMMER Forward Control long wheelbase chassis with standard cab and coach-built platform body...	419	0	0
21 gall. tank extra............................	3	0	0
Painting and Lettering........................	8	10	0
	430	10	0
Less-			
Allowance on 1934 Reo........................	120	0	0
	310	10	0
Tax to June 30th..............................	9	12	6
	£320	2	6

　　　Registration No:　　EBB.719.

　　　Chassis No:　　　　76654.

　　　Engine No:　　　　15861.

　　Guaranteed as per Manufacturers Printed
　　　　　Specification.

E.&.O.E.

The photograph may be of very poor quality but this is the only reminder of the Commer LN5 FBB 619 (on far left of shot). As per all the other Commers bought new by Ritchies, it was supplied through Minories Garage of Newcastle. The platform 4-5 tonner, chassis no. 85B 378 was purchased on 30th October 1937 at a total cost of £359-18s-6d. However as part of the War effort, it was impressed for purchase for Her Majesty's Forces on 24th September 1939 following the outbreak of World War II. The last Ritchies heard of this vehicle was when it was destroyed by fire – on the beaches of Dunkirk – to prevent it falling into German hands.

CHAPTER 4

World War II

On 3rd September 1939 (the day when Great Britain declared war on Germany) the Ritchie 13 strong fleet was a mix of six platform four wheelers plus seven four wheel tippers. Three of those with tipping bodies were the latest version in that an engine driven power take off discharged the cargo but the other four still required driver power to wind the tipping gear up by hand. Ernest and Norman had long favoured petrol – rather than diesel – powered vehicles although they'd still consider what was on offer. At the 1935 Royal Show held at the Town Moor at Newcastle, they were to inspect the latest Gardner powered ERFs, which were on display. Edwin Richard Foden was present trying to drum up sales and young Colin Ritchie had the pleasure of being lifted up into an ERF cab by Mr ER Foden himself. However, it would be almost another 40 years before Colin was to buy the ERF marque for the E&N Ritchie business.

SPEEDWAGON

Vehicle purchases during the 1930s had been something of a miscellany although by '39, the competitively priced Commer was being established as a Ritchie favourite. The Commers were usually supplied through Minories Garage, Jesmond Road, Newcastle and Ritchies were to get good, long-term service from this supplier. Minories were at least locally based because when there were any major problems with Ritchie's Vulcans, they had to be sent back to the manufacturer at Southport for repairs.

In mid February 1935, Hughie Race was to have three days paid holiday in the North West while his Vulcan – WM 9430 – was having work done on the engine and brakes. The Vulcan 2.5 tonner had come new to Ritchies in September 1933 and while it had the versatility to run both as a tipper and cattle wagon, it came with the hefty price tag of £526-6s-0d.

After being repaired, Hughie ran down to Liverpool and collected a total of 3 tons 7 cwt of bacon & dog biscuits. The rate for this load back to the North East was only £1 a ton and Ritchies had to pay 10% of the £3-7s to the Clearing House who provided the load. A note in the company ledgers records that Hughie's five days wages added up to £2-5s-10d (his four nights lodgings cost £1) while £1-11s-3d was spent on the 25 gallons of petrol used by the Vulcan which averaged 12mpg.

The Vulcans weren't known for their fast speed (it took Hughie 8.5 hours to travel the 175 miles back to Hetton) and quickest motor of the day was the aptly named Reo Speedwagon although it only returned 11mpg. At £399 – complete with cattle body – the 1934 Reo was also a lot cheaper than the Vulcan however it was to have a strange life. When only 15 months old, it was traded in to Minories against a new Commer and Ritchies were given £246 in part exchange. However, the dealer must have had problems selling it on because six months later – in September '35 – Ritchies bought the Reo back, but only for £205. It returned

Being allowed to buy a new commercial vehicle during World War II was not always possible but when Ritchies asked, they were allowed to purchase JTN 279. Delivered with a cheap built cab of utility style, the Thornycroft Sturdy 6 tonner – type ZE / TC 4 with chassis no. 30800 – was first registered on 2nd February 1942. With an unladen weight of 2 tons 17cwt, the road taxation excise licence then cost £35 per annum or £9-12s-6d, if bought for just three months. Used until August 1956, it had a new petrol engine fitted during April 1945. Driver Joe Wiseman (on left) shares the photograph with 'Uncle' Alan Robinson, who was always helping out at Ritchies and liked to travel with Joe. Alan Robinson was a relative of the Ritchie family and was to later make his mark – literally – in the panel beating motor trade. He was to lecture on the topic and also wrote a book on the subject. The bagged load is obviously from Casebourne cement being brought into the Ritchie yard for storage prior to onward distribution. Eagle eye observers will note the change in height of the Thornycroft headboard. This was done to accommodate the carriage of the demountable cattle boxes then used at Ritchies.

to Minories again in March '37 when it was traded in for a second time against a Commer 5 tonner.

LONG DISTANCE

With Ritchies only operating small capacity four wheelers, the modest tonnage rates available meant it wasn't really worth their while to travel excessive distances. But whenever they did, the two brothers would seem to spend hours planning the venture.

Back in October 1933, Jack Ferguson and Ralph Bleanch were to take the company's Bedford 2 tonner – BR 8878 – with a load of furniture across to Manchester. With a back load out of Silcock's only worth 12/- per ton, Ritchies only got £1-18s for the 3 tons 3 cwt they squeezed onto the little Bedford. While doing 14mpg, it still took nine hours for the Bedford to do the Liverpool to Hetton trip. However, getting £7-10s for the initial load of furniture, Ritchies actually made £5-3s nett profit on the run.

The company's first diesel powered vehicle – the Gardner 4LK powered Thornycroft Sturdy HBB 578 – didn't come into service until March 1939 and six months later was one of the newest vehicles on fleet. It was to come under the scrutiny of the Government Inspectors who were forcibly purchasing vehicles for the war effort. However with the Army fleet being standardised on petrol driven vehicles, there was no interest at all in the fairly new Thornycroft.

Originally, Ritchies had three vehicles impressed – the Commer four wheelers FBB 619, FVK 36 and GTN 257 – and all were driven out the yard on September 24th 1939 by Army personnel. A fourth vehicle – the three-month-old Fordson three-ton tipper HVK 991 – was impressed on January 26th 1940 and Hugh Race was instructed to drive that to Aldershot for subsequent Army use.

The British Expeditionary Force used all these vehicles but the only report, which Ritchies later received, related to FBB 619. It was driven well into France and was apparently to give faultless service. The only reason its performance was noted was the soldier who drove it, came from Stockton-on-Tees, which was then in County Durham. As the E&N Ritchie name and Hetton-le-Hole, County Durham address was still clearly painted on the door it obviously reminded him of home. That same soldier was still driving the Commer when it was used to evacuate the troops back through Dunkirk (in late May 1940) and the last he saw of it was when it was in flames on the beach: 'We were all told to destroy our vehicles,' he later told the Ritchie family, 'to stop them falling into enemy hands.'

ANDERSON SHELTERS

With the outbreak of war, the Government arranged for every family in the country to be issued with an Anderson bomb shelter. The families themselves would have to erect them but to Ritchies, this was to mean a huge amount of work delivering the shelters out from Hetton railway station.

George Kirkbride recalls the shelters were made up in sections and the number of pieces that were delivered would vary according to the size of the family: 'Everybody got the two end pieces – one with a door – and a ventilator – but if there only two people at the house, they'd only receive two of the big central arched sections. But if there were more at home then I was instructed to deliver another one or two more of the central sections.'

George recalls that humping the sharply edged sections over the back walls of the houses meant for heavy wear on his gloves and overalls, although last thing George would hand over was a plan of how the shelter had to be built: 'You had to dig a large hole wide enough for the arched sections and once you'd put the shelter together, the earth you dug out was used to cover the top over as much as possible.'

Everyone had a shelter although Kathleen Ritchie (as she was then called) recalls that both Ernest and Norman had second – larger – concrete shelters. Naturally Hetton Sand & Gravel were used for these constructions which were built by Hinchcliffe Hewitt & sons, the building contractors of nearby Haswell. These bigger shelters proved a haven for both the Ritchie family – and their near neighbours – although Kathleen recalls their one had a family of ducks living on the earth covered top. The subsequent air raids meant many nights were spent in the shelter although Kathleen says theirs suffered from flooding in bad weather and smoke fumes when the stove was lit.

George Kirkbride – and office man Tom Soulsby – were amongst the many who were called up for Wartime service in mid 1940. George had his call up deferred by two months because he'd passed his HGV driving test, by driving a loaded Commer 4 tonner round the streets of Sunderland to the examiner's satisfaction. The outbreak of war saw the requirement to pass the HGV test abolished until it was reinstated 30 years later.

The older, senior drivers like Matty Hall were initially exempted from military service although they were to be co-opted to work for the centrally controlled Ministry of War Transport. The three long distance men were based at Thirsk in North Yorkshire during the week and they were instructed where to go from there. A regular start off point on a Monday was to head for the Royal Ordnance Factory at Birtley for a load of ammunition for onward haulage to a barracks or ammo dump.

One memorable regular job for the new Thornycroft Sturdy was two return trips a week between Sunderland and Southampton carrying specially made wooden propellers for Short's Flying Boats (and bringing damaged ones back as a return load).

Back in the North East, airfield construction work meant that the produce of Hetton Sand & Gravel was in great demand. Depending on what was happening, when the weather was kind – especially during the summer months – the Ritchie tippers could be working literally night and day.

In the early part of the War, six of the remaining Ritchie vehicles were all earmarked for special duties. If required, the 5-ton Commer DTN 949 had to go straight to Martins Bank in Hetton and there assist with the removal of all the Bank's money. It was then planned to conceal this cash at a secret location. The small Guy – VK 4218 – and the Morris 2 tonner, UP 9518, were used as Fire Pumps with the Auxiliary Fire Service while two five ton Commer tippers were requisitioned for use by Durham County Council for the distribution of sand bags and other air raid protection materials. Last of the special duty vehicles was CTN 802, which in the event of invasion had to report to the Home Guard Centre, Lyons Buildings, Hetton and there assist – it's believed - with the evacuation of local dignitaries.

With petrol / diesel fuel being strictly rationed for use, the Ritchie haulage vehicles were also asked to cover the delivery of school meals from the central kitchen at Houghton-le-Spring (located in the Old Brewery) to about half a dozen schools in the Whitton Gilbert and Sacriston areas. Jack Delap had left school – on a Friday - at the age of 14 and started to work at Ritchies on the Saturday as a garage lad cum gofor. It seemed to be his job to find a driver to take the small Vulcan on the school meal round although in fairness he did have a vested interest in doing the run: 'George Irwin, the cattle wagon driver might do the run,' recalls Jack, 'although Matty Bell, one of the tipper drivers also did the job as well. After we delivered the meals to the final school, we were always given our lunch – which was far better than the bread & jam I might get if I was at home. We then had to retrace our route and collect the empty containers to take back to the Old Brewery.'

A slightly different aspect of the Ritchie work was when they were asked to supply agricultural tractors – again for the use of Durham County Council – for ploughing work, on a variety of land around the County. Rates for that work were fixed through the Agricultural War Committee and calculated per acre with light ploughing over stubble worth 15/- per acre. Best rates were for old pastures – at £1-10s per acre – while sowing, rolling and harrowing was worth 4/- per acre. The company notes reckoned that any light or medium ploughing could cover five acres in a day (with a three furrow plough) while fuel consumption was reckoned to be 1 gallon per hour.

Generally speaking, the early '40s was certainly a big revenue earning time for the Ritchies but all were pleased when 1945 – and peace – was finally reached.

The austere look of the depot with boarded up windows reflects the mood of the country during World War II. The lean-to blacksmith's shop can be seen attached to the rear of the building. A number of the Ritchie staff were to leave for wartime service in the Armed Forces including Tom Soulsby (seen left in later years) and George Kirkbride (above). On 6th April 1940, George was allowed home on leave long enough to marry his wife Margaret.

Bought just as World War II was coming to an end in July 1945, the Maudslay Mogul Mark II FUP 187 proved to be a tremendous servant to Ritchies. The vehicle has stood the test of time and is now part of the Ritchie preserved collection although its restoration is not quite fully complete. During its 20+ years of active service, it was normally driven by long serving driver Mathew Hall. Always seen wearing a cap, Matty was the epitome of a professional driver and was always prepared no matter what sort of load or situation he encountered. Even the first fall of snow would find Matty equipped with a shovel while his assorted equipment of ropes, chocks and wedges also included boot polish – to keep his boots clean. Such a tremendous character he was also known for his ability to give directions (to almost anywhere in the country) using Public Houses as markers. The horseshoe on the grille brought good luck to the Maudslay and its believed to have come from the Ritchie stable and the horse named Taffy. Long serving office worker Dorothy Dicken (as she was then) is seen with the Maudslay just after the vehicle was painted – and before its headlights were re-affixed.

MAUDSLAY MOGUL MARK II.

JULY 23 Purchased through Motor. Distributors Ltd, Leeds

MAUDSLAY 'MOGUL MARK II' diesel engined chassis

fitted with

A.E.C. 7.7. Litre Engine   Engine No. A173/4700.

Five speed overdrive gearbox   CHASSIS. 11401

36" x 8" Tyres

Standard Cab and Flat.

Cab "J" TYPE NO 118 with two door keys M.RN. 11

Servo. Trailer. Brake. equipment

24 VOLT. Lighting and Starting

6¾ TO 1 FINAL. DRIVE RATIO.

All to Standard. specification.   (In Grey)

Complete with tool kit and spare wheel.

NUMBER PLATES. FUP 187.

M.O.W.T. LICENCE. NO. 74715.

CHASSIS NO. 11401.   CLAYTON DEWANDRE SERVO

ENGINE NO. 4700.   TYPE WH3-175 10819

GEARBOX NO 1449   SERVO No 693

FRONT AXLE NO. 368. (KIRKSTALL MAKE)

REAR AXLE NO 366.

	T	C	Q	LBS		
UNLADEN. WEIGHT,	4 —	10 —	0 —	74.		
	FEET	INS.			FEET	INS.
LENGTH OF BODY.				WIDTH OF BODY		

Oswald. Tillotson Ltd   Samson Engineering Works

Preston Street   Bradford.

First day at work Oct 10th 1945.

Continued overleaf.

39

ROAD HAULAGE ASSOCIATION
LIMITED.

This is to Certify that

Messrs. E. &. N. Ritchie,

OF Triumph Garage, Station Road, Hetton le Hole, Co. Durham.

WAS THIS DAY ELECTED A MEMBER OF

ROAD HAULAGE ASSOCIATION

Dated this 1st day of January, 1945

Chairman.

Member of the Council.

Director.

Registered No. 6384

ARTICLE 13 (e) PROVIDES THAT :—

"If the Member's subscription shall be in arrear and unpaid for three months after the same shall have become due and a resolution for the removal of such Member shall have been passed by the National Council after consultation with the Area Committee of the Area in which such Member is a Member. Any Member in respect of whom any such resolution is passed shall ipso facto and immediately cease to be a Member and shall not be entitled to claim a return of any money paid by such Member to the Association by way of subscription call or donation."

This Certificate is the property of the Road Haulage Association Limited and must be surrendered to the Association on cessation of Membership.

Due to a reorganisation of the Road Haulage Association, E&N Ritchie were re-certified as being a member on 1st January 1945. And they've been an RHA member ever since.

CHAPTER 5

Bulls and Horses

Being such a small family business, it was always a big occasion whenever a new vehicle was bought. It got to be something of a ritual that at least one member of the Ritchie family would make the trip to the dealers – or even factory – to be given those new set of keys for the very first time. Naturally during the wartime years, most new Ritchie arrivals were very much second hand and acquired almost as a necessity to keep the business going. The company had to make an application through the Ministry of War Transport for a permit to buy a new four-wheeler. And at the time, Ritchies were also restricted in the manufacturer they could buy from. They were given a list of three – Guy, Maudslay and Dennis – and while their choice was Guy, the authorities issued a permit for the purchase of a new Maudslay.

The Mark II Mogul FUP 187 was collected from the Midlands on July 23rd 1945. Amongst the entourage that drove down to the Midlands was 16-year-old Colin Ritchie. While the North East had suffered serious bomb damage during the war, this was almost insignificant compared to the damage which Coventry endured. Colin had never seen destruction like this before and the images he saw were to stay with him for the rest of his life.

Maudslay Motor Co was amongst the many engineering factories in Coventry that had been badly hit by the German bombers. As part of their strategy to try and avoid

being targeted, the company had erected a shadow factory in the countryside at Castle Maudslay near Alcester. However, due to the damage suffered at HQ, vehicle production was eventually moved the 30 miles or so to Alcester. Although on this trip, the Ritchie collection crew had to visit both Maudslay centres - first to collect the paperwork and then to collect the vehicle.

ANODITE

Although it was late July when the new Maudslay got back to Hetton-le-Hole, it didn't go into service until 10th October 1945. Such a large gap between accepting delivery of a new vehicle and actually starting to use it was fairly routine at Ritchies for many years.

After first being suggested by Norman Ritchie, it became standard policy until well into the 1960s, that any vehicle (although second hand ones weren't given such extensive treatment) had as much of the unseen metal work protected with a material called Anodite. Manufactured by Goodlass Wall & Co Ltd (established in 1840 at Liverpool, London and branches) the rust preventing composition was very much like red lead in appearance.

The garage staff at Ritchies would remove things like bumpers and all the bright work possible so the Anodite could be laid on thickly to the metal underneath. Even rubber mats were removed from the cab interior so the Anodite could be applied to the cab floor and generally enhance the life expectancy of the vehicle.

This was a job that was done between other work in the garage and while it was company policy to apply all the paint by hand, Ronnie Kirtley (a trainee mechanic at the time) recalls trying to save a lot of time by later spraying the Anodite on. 'We first had to apply an aluminium spirit sealer but the Anodite was really thick like shipyard paint. It was really slow going so Roy Todd and I decided to take turns working down the chassis with the spray gun. I think it saved time but Roy and I suffered lead poisoning by breathing in the Anodite droplets and the next day we both suffered from diarrhoea – so we never tried that trick again.'

Although the Mogul II came with a cab (not every vehicle of the era had one fitted by the manufacturer) and a platform body, Ritchies had long favoured Joseph Bailey & Sons of East Rainton, Co Durham as their favoured body builders. The Ritchie vehicles had three coats of paint as standard – one. undercoat, two of gloss – with the two-tone colour match being Dulux Brilliant Green and Deep Brunswick Green. Baileys also did the sign writing.

KHAKI ELECTION

The immediate post war period was a strange time for the country in general and Ritchies too were to see a great deal of internal movement. First reverberations were felt after the so called Khaki Election of 1945, when the war winning feat of Winston Churchill was quickly forgotten as Clement Attlee's Labour Government was swept into power. Their mandate of creating Government ownership of a mass of services saw the coalmines taken over into the National Coal Board (NCB) and the National Health Service (NHS) created.

Perhaps of more importance to the road haulage world was Labour's promise of nationalising road transport. During the war, the Ministry of War Transport (MOWT) had shown how co-ordinated use of goods vehicles could be of huge benefit to the country. The Labour leaders perhaps didn't fully appreciate that during the exceptional circumstances of a World War, the whole of the country would want to pull together. Those feelings would not apply during peacetime when Free Enterprise created competition, but such details were not to prevent the Road Haulage Executive creating the huge structure of British Road Services.

Unless you endured this period yourself, it's hard to imagine the anguish such plans were to cause. Norman Ritchie in particular took the prospect of losing all his vehicles into Government ownership very badly. And while time was to eventually show that Ritchies could claim exemption from compulsory purchase of their vehicles, this didn't prevent many sleepless nights for the Ritchie family.

It perhaps helped their cause to stay free that Ritchies had never really expanded into larger vehicles carrying more freight over longer distances. That step could have made them a huge fish in the North East pond of transport although Ernest and Norman couldn't always agree on taking that big step into expansion.

Joining the garage staff in 1945 was John Smiles. He'd been a good friend of Colin Ritchie for many years and both had gone to Houghton Grammar School together. But even during his school days, John would join Colin on a weekend at the Ritchie depot helping out as best he could.

John recalled a natural rapport with Norman Ritchie: 'We just seemed to click,' said John, 'and I got on very well with Norman all the time I worked there.' John was to build a great reputation as being a good mechanic amongst the Ritchie staff and said it was probably down to the ability of being good at diagnosis: 'Being able to work out where the fault was seemed to be a strength of mine,' said John, 'although in the post war years, you had to make do and

With an unladen weight of 2 tons 15cwt 3qrs, Commer produced these very light tippers rated to carry 4-5 tons loads. EUP 863 was bought new from Minories Garage on 14th February 1942 although didn't go on the road until 1st June. With chassis no. 15A6420, the Commer Superpoise was equipped with Edbro hydraulic tipping gear and body. By the time driver Jack Delap (above) was given the vehicle, it had been totally refurbished (in house). As the norm in those days (when weighbridges were in short supply) all the Ritchie tippers were certified by the Weights & Measures authority on the cubic capacity of their bodies. In that way, it was an easy calculation to work out the weight – and quantity - of the load. As an indicator of such capacity, lead seals and markers were placed on the body. Jack would

often run between the quarry and the Ritchie yard ferrying in materials for the Sand & Gravel plant and whenever he did this job, he always had to return to the quarry with a billy can of tea for Jackie Teasdale: 'If I did 10 loads,' said Jack, 'then Jackie got 10 cans of tea from the ice cream shop. That's all he lived on.' Those other Commers ran by Ritchies with the Bendix cable brakes are recalled as awful to stop. Quarry man Jackie Teasdale had an agreement with the gateman (who used to man the White Gates mineral line railway crossing near what is now the Hetton Cricket Club) to give him precedence: 'If you see me coming down the hill loaded,' Jackie told him, 'you had better stop the train as I won't be able to pull up if you close those gates.'

mend. And just coming up with good ideas on how to repair something – when you couldn't get the relevant spares – was how you survived.'

John recalled some very good mods he did with the braking systems on some of the Commers: 'They were rated for say 10 tons gross and we'd load them to 14 tons so naturally the drivers would complain the brakes weren't up to the job. I remember fitting free moving brake shoes to the Bendix cable brakes and this greatly improved the braking. I suppose I should have patented that idea.'

As well as spares, vehicles were in short supply and John recalls a pair of ex military Thornycroft search light vehicles which came: 'They had the engine under the cab because they had a huge generator under the bonnet. We took the generators out and fitted them with hydraulic tipper bodies and they worked for a couple of years like that.' Hardest time that John recalls was the winter of 1947: 'The cold and snow seemed to last for months,' he said. 'The sand & gravel plant would literally seize up solid and the only way we could free the ice was if we put some old tyres underneath the drum and set fire to them.'

The end of hostilities in 1945 was to eventually see those staff that had left to fight, return to take up their jobs. Naturally the War was to leave its mark on many of them and George Kirkbride recalls his experience meant that he wasn't satisfied in simply resuming his driving job at Ritchies: 'The war had given me some responsibility and made me realise there was more to life than just wagon driving,' he says. George was to eventually make a career with the NCB while office man Tom Soulsby was to leave his high office desk at Ritchies when he changed direction to take up school teaching.

Staying slightly longer were both Tommy White and Joe Garland. Jack Delap – who was still a teenager at the time – recalls that Tommy had been a prisoner of war (POW) and been forced to walk right across Italy before being imprisoned: 'This meant he

was left with a permanent limp,' says Jack. Joe Garland had served his time in the RAF and he was to proudly wear his old uniform even when he was driving again at Ritchies: 'I remember Joe always had his hair slicked back and he liked to be known as one of the Brylcream Boys,' says Jack.

CONTINUOUS CROSSLEY

Jack himself went away for his two years National Service (from 1948-50) but one thing which didn't change in his absence, was the performance of the company's static Crossley engine, that had originally been bought when the plant was built in 1934. Housed in a tin shed behind the garage, the two stroke Crossley operated a system of belts which in turn operated the mechanism for the Ritchie (Hetton Sand & Gravel) crushing & grading equipment.

In charge of this plant was Jackie Teasdale (who must have been founder Ralph Ritchie's first ever employee) although it required a huge joint effort to breath life into the engine – especially during the winter. 'It had a massive starting handle,' says Jack Delap, 'and while two on the handle and perhaps another couple pulling on one of the belts might do the trick in the summer, in the winter a special cold start trick was required. Jackie would remove a plug from the engine and drop in a lighted rope, which was smouldering. He'd then fill a sauce bottle full of petrol and pour it into the cylinder, so the combined effort of the petrol exploding and those on the handle and belt pulling would be enough to cough the engine into life. If it did fire, you had to try and pull the starting handle free or if not, make sure you kept out of its way – it could be lethal. But give the Crossley its due, once started it would run all day and was of little bother.'

His return from National Service saw Jack promoted from garage gofor to driver and the first motor he was given was a small 1942 Commer tipper: 'The body on this vehicle – like all the company tippers – had

44

a lead marking to certify that when full it was carrying a specific number of cubic yards.'

Loading the various grades of gravel in the yard was done under hoppers. The material had been brought to Hetton for cleaning & grading (from the company's various quarries at Fallowfield, Easington, Haswell etc) but all had been hand shovelled into the crusher / grader by Billy White: 'It was a hard job but Billy seemed to enjoy it.'

Whenever Jack had to collect yellow sand, it meant a visit to the NCB quarry at Hetton Downs – and the prospect of hand loading himself: 'It was a special sort of sand,' he says. 'I used to take it the 40 miles to the reservoir being built at Cowshill in Weardale - I think they needed it for the water filtration plant up there.'

ADMIN

While most of the activity in the Ritchie organisation was very much at ground level, administering affairs were done from the first floor offices. As Norman was very much a hands on guy, it was Ernest Ritchie that ruled the roost upstairs. The late Dorothy Dicken was to take over the office admin after Tom Soulsby joined up and in 1945, she was joined by Audrey Earnshaw (later to become Audrey Maughan) who was then only 15 years old.

Audrey recalls that her working hours was 9am-6pm (with an hour for her to cycle back home for lunch) although just like the rest of the Ritchie staff, working a bit of overtime – to get that urgent letter into the post – was often taken for granted. Audrey recalls some happy times in her four years at Ritchies although in all that time, she always referred to her two bosses either as Mr Ernest or Mr Norman: 'In fact when I left Ritchies and went to work for the Northern Bus Company,' she said, 'I found it very strange that the management there expected that I should simply call them by their first name. I felt a bit uncomfortable

because I'd been used to using the Mr prefix at Ritchies.'

Being the office junior, it was often Audrey's job to re-tax all the vehicles and this meant a bus ride to Durham City for a visit to the taxation department at Shire Hall. Another regular bus ride saw Audrey go in the opposite direction to Sunderland: 'With petrol still being rationed,' she said, 'we had to collect coupons from whoever we sold the petrol to. But when we wanted to buy petrol, I had to take those coupons – and a cheque – to the Petroleum Board at Sunderland docks so the petrol could be paid for before it was delivered.' The suggestion that such monthly trips were an excuse for a day out in Sunderland was given short shrift: 'Not really,' said Audrey. 'Mr Ernest knew exactly how much time I should take for the return journey so I obviously couldn't skive.'

LONG DISTANCE LIVESTOCK

By 1950, the Ritchie Thornycroft HBB 578 (new in 1939) had covered a huge mileage and had come unscathed through the war. However, it was still disappointing when it snapped its crankshaft so it was taken into the Gardner agents in Newcastle – Painters – where the engine was re-built with a new block and crankshaft.

When due consideration was given to this failure it was recalled that not long after new (10 years earlier in 1940) driver Matty Hall had reported a strange change to the engine note. Because of the high regard in which the Ritchie brothers felt of Matty's judgement, it was decided to get a load for Manchester and take the vehicle to Gardners for investigation. With wartime constraints applying, it's recalled a repair was done (with the engine in situ) and while Gardners wouldn't say what they'd done, they assured the driver it would be all right. It would seem the engine was then run for 10 years with an – almost - broken crankshaft: 'It was used on MOWT work during the war,' says Jack, 'and I think

In 1950, the much travelled 1939 Thornycroft received a new lease – and a new role - in life when it was re-equipped with this brand new box built by Joseph Bailey & Sons. When originally bought – in 1939 – the vehicle arrived at Hetton in chassis / scuttle fashion. It was sent to Northern Coachbuilders (who were also the Reo dealership) in Newcastle for the original cab and body to be added. The timber used by Baileys for the box is believed to have been some very rare New Zealand Pywana Pine. It's pictured (above) on General Trade Plates before it was re-taxed to go back on the road. Although it looks very substantial, the horse / bull box only weighed 2 tons 2 quarters which give the Thornycroft – in this guise – a tare weight of 4 tons 17cwt 1qr. Extremely light in 21st century terms, it was extremely slow – even in 1950. On long distance runs to places like Reading, regular driver Jack Delap (seen on the left - with fellow driver Joe Wiseman) was the butt of many jokes thrown in his direction by other livestock crews. These easily overtook the slow moving Sturdy although Jack recalls his time with the Thornycroft at Ritchies with great pleasure. Stuart Ritchie's earliest memory of the Thornycroft was when – as a seven year old – he accompanied his father to Potts Farm at Elemore Lane in Pittington. 'All I had to do was stand at the corner of the wagon and shoo the lambs up the ramp as my Dad and the farmer drove the flock out the field,' said Stuart. 'But on seeing the first lambs come round the corner, I took fright and ran up the road – and of course all the lambs followed me. It took ages for them to be rounded up again.'

C & M. Ritchie

DISTRIBUTORS OF

HUMBER   HILLMAN   COMMER   KARRIER

THE
MINORIES GARAGES Ltd.
—— PERKINS DEISELS LTD.——

PHONES: JESMOND 2000 (5 LINES) DARLINGTON 5291-2 (2 LINES)   AND AT NORTHGATE DARLINGTON

JESMOND ROAD
NEWCASTLE-UPON-TYNE 2

MINORIES EXCHANGE ENGINES - ROOTES GROUP PRODUCTS.

ALL ENGINES COMPLETELY REBUILT TO A HIGH STANDARD OF ENGINEERING
SPECIFICATION.

1. Cylinder block rebored or resleeved as necessary.
2. New pistons fitted.
3. Crankshaft re-ground, all journals.
4. New main and connecting rod bearings.
5. New valves, valve springs and tappets as necessary.
6. New timing chain and tensioner.
7. Water pump overhauled, new bushes, spindle and gland washers
   as necessary.
8. Flywheel starter ring replaced if necessary.
9. Completely reconditioned clutch unit.
10. Oil pump reconditioned, new pump gear replaced and oil release
    valve replaced.

Type of Engine.....*Commer LH5*.......
Price excluding fitting.......*£60 : 0 : 0.*

Service Engine. 960   *MC*

CONDITIONS OF SALE.

        The reconditioned engine is sold only subject to the following
conditions :-

1. That the engine is free of all broken or damaged parts in block
   or cylinder head.
2. That the cylinder block will regrind or re-sleeve (extra charge
   when re-sleeving is necessary).
3. That the crankshaft will re-grind to a minimum of .040 oversize.
4. That the engine bearers are free from damage or fracture.

        I/We note conditions as above and agree to meet the cost of
any new replacement parts as necessary in addition to the standard
charge of a replacement engine.

Fitted to EVK496

Sgd.........................
....   *Jany 28/1949.*

48

Ralph Bleanch also drove it for a time but it hardly missed a beat.' Although livestock transport had been a big Ritchie activity during the '20s and '30s, by 1950, the company only one had demountable cattle container left: 'It was parked in the yard supported on four oil drums,' says Jack Delap, 'and there was a tripod style of block and tackle which you used when you wanted to lift the box onto the back of a flat wagon.'

Cattle work did take the Thornycroft – and its new driver Jack Delap – to Hexham, Berwick and as far south as the mart in York, but a slightly different class of livestock was to be moved when Ritchies got into transporting horses and bulls. 'The first horses we did were just locally for people involved in the Point to Point sort of socialising activity,' says Jack, 'but as we got more involved, we began to carry horses for folk in the racing game.'

Strangely, the big movers in this business were vehicles operated by the local railways – the LNER: 'Rather than just use a demountable box,' says Jack, 'the Thornycroft was taken back to Baileys and had a special horsebox built onto it. When re-painted, it certainly looked the business – and certainly better than the LNER boxes.' Jack travelled as far north as Edinburgh while the racecourse near Ayr was also a regular destination: 'If I had three horses on for a weekend meet, I was booked into a bed and breakfast for the whole stay. I never felt inclined to put a bet on although I would always help the stable lad and perhaps lead the horses out around the parade ring.'

In 1951, Jack was to lead the Agar Khan's horse named something like Tulia and this was to go on and win the St Ledger at Doncaster. While the big grey 'Mr Watt' – a subsequent winner of the Grand National – was also handled a few time by the Delap / Thornycroft combination.

When not carrying racehorses, the Thornycroft was used to transport prize bulls from Wesley Weightman's farm at Copt Hill to Reading: 'They went down there for auction and I would always help Sam the herdsman, because the bulls had to be washed & shampooed so they looked their best prior to the sale. We used baby oil on them to make their skin glisten – they often fetched prices measured in thousands of guineas. And even though they weighed about two tons each, they were quite docile – unless they got the scent from a cow nearby and then they might get frisky.'

Jack and the Thornycroft seemed well suited to this style of work although it required a lot of patience: 'I'd load perhaps three bulls at 5am and we wouldn't get to Reading until 7pm,' he says. 'The Thornycroft was pretty slow and would only do about 32mph but you had to be careful you didn't hurt the beasts going round corners too fast. And sometimes, Sam would need me to stop and perhaps take the bulls out – but only if we found a field and the farmer would give us permission.'

Perhaps the biggest bonus was when Jack and the herdsman would sleep overnight in the Luton top of the body: 'Once we put the small interior light out, the beasts would settle down and the heat they gave off meant you were never cold during the winter. It was better than central heating.' This internal heat contrasted greatly with the lack of heat in the Thornycroft cab: 'I'd always take off the fan belt during the winter and I'd also often run with the engine side panels off,' says Jack, 'but the top and bottom of it was the Gardner engine never gave off much heat. And you could almost fall out of the cab with the noise – it was that bad.'

Jack was to eventually leave Ritchies and later make a career with Pickfords Heavy Haulage. But little did he think that 50 years later, the same Thornycroft would still be on the Active list at Ritchies – and still as slow and cold to drive.

Mr Ernest – as he was known to differentiate him from Mr Norman or later, Mr Colin – is seen with the office staff of January 1948. On the left is Dorothy Dicken (later McArdle) and on the right is Audrey Earnshaw (later Maughan). In the background is the Thornycroft 'Sturdy' tipper HUP 621. With chassis number 27811, this was purchased through the Oswald Tillotson dealership at Bradford. It had the War Department number of 170667 as originally the Ministry of Supply bought it.

Although bought in 1947, this Chaseside loading shovel was not registered – JUP 137 – until June 1950. Chaseside Engineering Ltd had offices both at Hertford and Failsworth, Manchester. Described as having a bulldozer attachment and a half cubic yard size of bucket, its model name was a Demon Light Excavator. It was used for loading duties until 1958 (when it was traded in against a new Weatherill loading shovel) and is pictured when new having Anodite applied to its chassis by Jackie Teasdale. In the background are Ritchie's old stables and also the small Koop carts. These were used by horses like Taffy to deliver small consignments of sand & gravel around Hetton. Apparently the horses could tell when they were being loaded as to whether they had reached their full weight. They would indicate this to the driver (by moving on or going back) that they either had enough – or had room for more.

CHAPTER 6

The Next Generation

Colin Ritchie was educated at Houghton-le-Spring Grammar School and the flair he showed in the subjects of history, geography and mathematics led the staff there to believe that young Mr Ritchie had the right material to become a school teacher himself. A quiet spoken and unassuming sort of guy, Colin was to only show passion in a subject if he was 100% interested in it. And while the prospect of a career in teaching was not something that was to excite him, the inherited ability in engineering had been apparent – and utilised - for some time.

On leaving school in 1945, he signed up for a five-year apprenticeship with the specialist engine concern of Ferriers. Based at Byker in Newcastle, this company overhauled all manner of engines and while the staff there were obviously highly trained engineers, the talents of apprentice Ritchie were to be sought after by one famous Newcastle haulier. 'Jakey Adams – JR Adams – had some Vulcans with Perkins engines which ran on the trunk to Manchester,' recalls Colin's eldest son Stuart. 'My Dad always told me that Jakey would pester him to try and enhance the Perkins output. I suppose getting an apprentice to do that was cheaper than one of the fully qualified Ferriers engineers but it was an obvious compliment as to what Jakey thought of my Dad.'

Having to attend evening classes at College on a night meant Colin was to have little social life although taking the bus to work in Newcastle every morning saw him meet up with his wife to be - Sylvia Robinson - who rode that same bus into town. Sylvia soon discovered she had to share her life with wagons, as even on a weekend, Colin would be down at the Ritchie garage crawling under something or other. Although even this dedicated man allowed himself to have Saturday night off.

INTO THE GARAGE

Colin was to do his two years National Service with the Royal Air Force and back at Hetton-le-Hole, he moved into the Ritchie garage to join his Uncle Norman. This gave Norman more time to develop his salesman technique as sales of cars (mainly of Morris manufacture) were an important part of the Ritchie business.

The family had big plans to expand and applied for planning permission to build a petrol station on Houghton Road. The planners thought (wrongly) that Ritchies intended to base their road fleet there and wouldn't give them permission but strangely neither Ernest nor Norman wanted to pursue the application on appeal.

Ritchies also applied to modernise their HQ at Triumph Garage by building a drive through style of filling station (underneath the first floor offices) but this too was refused by the local planners. All that was allowed was for the fitting of electric fuel pumps and a new frontage to the premises.

At the rear of the premises, Ritchies expanded their warehousing to accommodate storage for bagged cement.

Ritchies two Proctors were bought second hand on 18th August 1952 from their first owners, Washington Chemical Co Ltd. HUP 135 was chassis no. 470511 and was first registered on 4th September 1947. JPT 199 had chassis no. 471118 and was new on 15th March 1948. Both ran on 34 x 7 tyres with body sizes of 16'5" long and 7'5" wide. Both were powered by the Perkins P6 engine although JPT was to have a new exchange engine fitted on 9th September 1953. This was supplied through North Eastern Motors of Newcastle at a cost of £140. A discount of 10% was given although Ritchies had to pay £6-6s-6d for delivery. The driver in front of HUP 135 is Bobby Robson who was apparently taken prisoner during the early part of World War II but escaped and returned home via Switzerland. He then went back into France during the D Day landings.

Regular loads were brought into Hetton from Casebourne Cement, the long established producer from Haverton Hill on Teesside. Long before builders merchants like Travis Perkins offered home delivery, Hetton Sand & Gravel would also deliver small amounts of sand, gravel and cement to domestic customers.

The Casebourne loads were recalled as being a great load to collect as the nice clean bags were slowly delivered to the driver by means of a mobile conveyor belt. This contrasted with the bagged cement collected from the Wylam Wharf at Sunderland.

This fleet line up around 1953 sees the two Proctors take centre stage. So far as Ritchies were concerned these two 6 tonners were probably quite big motors for the time. However, by the time they came to Hetton-le-Hole, the Proctor business was in retraction. Built by Proctor Springwood Ltd at their works in Mousehold near Norwich, the vehicles were only produced between 1947 and 1952. The lightweight 5-6 tonner was apparently styled on the similar Seddon and Vulcan four wheelers of the period. Fitted with Moss gearbox and axles, the one recalled idiosyncrasy of the Proctor was that the speedometer worked from right to left – which is the opposite direction to every other speedometer then in service.

Brought up the North Sea from the Cement Marketing Company's plant at Northfleet in Kent by a small coaster, a rough sea journey could mean that many of the cement paper bags were split open. And if you were handling such a load – in the rain and wind – it meant every part of you got covered in that grey powder.

COAL ROUND

Handballing your load on and off had long been a way of life to wagon drivers – and driver's mates. It wasn't too bad if you were simply handling bottles of HP Sauce (an early regular load collected at Hetton railway station) but some of the other weights you were expected to handle would make the modern day Health & Safety Executive cringe. It helped if you were a huge guy like Ralph Bleanch but even smaller frames like Jack Delap can recall being expected to move 16 stone bags of wheat – yes 2cwt – all by himself.

Things were set to change as the Ritchie

records from 16th November 1954 marked a red-letter day. 'This is the first load under a new system,' the record states. 'The 6 tons 15cwt load of 1,440 bricks, were loaded onto Thornycroft LPT 461 at the Ferens & Love works in Cornsay and transported the 30 miles to the South Durham Iron Works at West Hartlepool. They were loaded by forklift and the bricks were supported on six pallets with 240 bricks on each pallet.'

Never have so few words heralded such a change in working practices although in one aspect of the Ritchie business, that handballing effort would still be long required. Back in 1934, Ernest and Norman had started up a domestic coal round, as something for the sand & gravel vehicles & drivers to do during what should have been the quieter months (for building) of winter. Coal was collected from the railway sidings at Barton Street coal yard and delivered – in bags - to houses round Hetton.

Not every driver liked being given this job because, as well as the dirt and the awkward carrying of loaded sacks on your

The Ritchie Weatherill (below) was bought on 23rd January 1958 with hire purchase through the Southern Industrial Trust. Supplied by the Newcastle Ford dealership of RH Patterson & Co Ltd, the loading shovel was based on a Fordson Diesel Major tractor chassis and is recalled as being a fairly reliable machine. With chassis no. 2 HCS A/822, it was used in the Ritchie yard (by all and sundry) for loading vehicles and had three quarters of a cubic yard capacity. If needs be, it was also driven by road to the local Ritchie quarries. It was also later converted into a forklift when Ritchies got the job of removing a large amount of railway sleepers. The company's Smith Super 10 excavator (machine no. 24146) went into Ritchie service on 3rd May 1956 and tipped the scales at 10 tons 4cwt 3qrs. Like their smaller 1954 Smith's 8 excavator, it remained at the Ritchie Fallowfield quarry site. Both these tracked machines were collected new from the Smith factory – and transported to County Durham – by the Consett heavy haulier, Siddle C Cook.

shoulders to be dropped into more awkward coalhouses, you were also responsible for collecting the money from the householder.

Bob Scott was recalled as being a dedicated coal man and was actually very protective of his round. He also had a practiced eye at simply being able to look at a pile of coal and say whether it was good enough for him to load and sell on. The coal round job was to be made a lot easier after E&N Ritchie, became the first independent coal merchant to operate an Autobagger (the National Coal Board did of course operate this type of vehicle) but that wasn't for many years to come. Up until then, the weighing and loading – before carrying and delivering - of each individual bag was just a way of life.

BUSY TIPPERS

The coal round seemed to have a life of its own as once established, the workload of Hetton Sand & Gravel vehicles could be hectic. Ritchie sourced materials were used to build the Sherburn Road Council housing estate near Durham City, while most of the Fulwell suburb of Sunderland was again down to Hetton S&G. Sunderland's Royal Infirmary was also built of Ritchie materials while perhaps the family's greatest claim to (building) fame is how the slipways on Doxford's shipyard – where the biggest ship on the Wear was launched – was again constructed with their materials. It's perhaps a shame that no one ever counted the number of journeys made by the Ritchie vehicles because they were extremely busy.

The Ritchie fleet was increased – overnight – with the purchase of a job lot from Washington Chemical Co Ltd in August 1952. Amongst that buy were four Muir-Hill, rear steer dumpers that went to work for Hetton Sand & Gravel. Although only of small capacity, they proved ideal to potter around the quarry or when the twice-yearly chore of clearing out the silt from the bottom of the yard's settling pond was required.

George Williams came to Ritchies not long after leaving school at Christmas 1949 because he'd always wanted to be a mechanic. Before he left the company employ in 1973, he was to enjoy a varied workload and driving the little Muir-Hills round the yard was something of a change compared to the daily garage life: 'They were ideal,' recalled George, 'but you had to be careful when tipping out the contents.' The length of travel of how far the dumper bucket would go over was controlled by a length of chain: 'But if the chain was out of adjustment and the bucket went over too far,' said George, 'it could bang against the rubber stops and the weight of sticky, silting mass inside was often enough, to throw the driver off balance and catapult him over the top of the machine – honestly.'

George was to be gifted with a mechanic's ability although he recalls having a hard taskmaster as a foreman when he started: 'Bill Dickinson had served his time with Ferriers the engine people at Newcastle. He knew his stuff but he was a hard guy to work for. I got on better with Harold Cheetham and John Smiles who had just finished their time.'

For his first week's pay as an apprentice, George received £1-5s which was actually the same weekly remuneration he was paid – in July 1956 – when he went into the Royal Air Force (at the age of 21) to do his National Service. By the time he got into the Services, George had learnt a lot in his time at Ritchies.

PERKINS PROCTOR

First memorable big job for George was to help out with the refurbishment of the 1939 Thornycroft four-wheeler, which Ralph Bleanch had looked after so well during World War II and was being converted for horse and bull transport. The Gardner 4LK engine was fully stripped down but to refurbish the cab, the carpentry talents of John 'Paddy' Kinnely were utilised: 'He was an Irish lad who was self employed,' said George, 'but he did a great job with the cab.'

The Thornycroft was well liked and did a

huge work load for Ritchies but George has different memories about the two four wheeled Proctors that came with the Washington Chemicals job lot: 'They had the Perkins P6 engine,' said George, 'and compared to the Gardner, they were a dirty engine that leaked oil all over the place.'

The Proctor could also be an awful vehicle to get started on a cold morning: 'I think the P6 only had one heater plug,' recalled George, 'which wasn't that successful. The best way to start these engines was to lift the bonnet cover and take the air filter off. You then dipped a rag in diesel and set it alight before dropping it down the air filter vent. Put your foot right down on the throttle and turning the engine over was enough to get it going, but you ended up being covered in soot from the burning rag. It was a right shambles.'

George actually did a three day trip down to London with one of these Proctors: 'I was on a week's holiday and with nothing else to do, the driver asked if I fancied a ride out with him.' Sleeping in the cab was a way of life then – for some – while George also got a drive: 'I told him I didn't even have a car licence but the lad said it was alright. I must have driven 10 miles out of London the day we'd unloaded.'

The Proctor is recalled as being a cramped, uncomfortable and rattler of a motor, while George recalls another time when he had to drive one back after a local breakdown: 'The selectors on the gearbox went so I removed the top casing and actually changed the gears by moving the selectors by hand.'

The Ritchie love of the small four-wheeler, however, was set to change with the arrival of the first six wheeler in the late '50s. While the early 1960s also saw the company share allegiances with their beloved Commer as the marque of AEC established a foothold.

Rated as having a 5-ton capacity, this Austin tipper had an unladen weight of 2 tons 16cwt. OPT 558 was new into service during July 1953 and it was fitted with the Perkins P6 engine, which always proved difficult to start. Usually driven by Joe Bleanch (although this isn't Joe at the steering wheel) it shares the photograph with office worker Mary Havelock (later Hall) who came to Ritchies straight from school. The Austin is recalled as being the first Ritchie motor to have a two-speed axle, which in itself proved troublesome in operation.

The petrol engine Thornycroft Sturdy LPT 461 was model type ZE/ER 4 and first registered on 28th April 1950. It shares the photograph with Johnny Smiles – on the left – and Alan Robinson. Due to the relatively poor quality of petrol at the time, it was a regular job of the Ritchie mechanics to de-coke the Thornycroft engines and grind the valves in. However for any bigger overhauls, close attention was needed. The cast iron engines are recalled as having alloy pistons and because these two metals heated up at different speeds, it was apparently quite easy to seize the engine when fitting new pistons. 'We had to run the engine for a half a day,' recalled George Williams, 'and keep squirting Redex upper cylinder lubricant into the carburettor. It caused clouds of smoke in the garage but it was something we had to do in order to bed them in right.'

Joe Bleanch seems happy with his brand new Commer QX 7 ton tipper, which went into service on 30th April 1957. Fitted with Telehoist tipping gear, it came direct from Commer complete with body of 6 cubic yards capacity. With 9'7" wheelbase, chassis no. 81A 1634 had an unladen weight of 3 tons 14cwt and is recalled both for its phenomenal performance and its long-term reliability. The six-cylinder petrol engine was apparently fitted with chrome cylinder liners and based on the engine used in the Humber Staff Car of war time years.

FERRIERS (NEWCASTLE) LTD.

MOTOR ENGINEERS.

TELEPHONE 56005, Two Lines
Private 63252 and 54898.
Telegrams FERRIERS 56005, Newcastle.

DIRECTORS { J. FERRIER.
{ K.A.T.FERRIER.
{ J.N.FERRIER.

Millers Road,
Of Shields Road,

NEWCASTLE on TYNE. 6.

Mr. Colin Ritchie,
"Sandylaw",
Hetton-le-Hole,
Co. Durham.

YOUR REF. _____   OUR REF. JNF/GF   2nd February, 1951

TO WHOM IT MAY CONCERN

    The above named has been in our employ since leaving secondary school at the age of 16 years.

    He has completed with us a five years indentured apprenticeship which terminated in September, 1950, and has since been employed as an engine fitter.

    He has proved to be an excellent workman in every respect, having had experience in the operation of machine tools and centre lathe work including screwing.

    We have found him to be industrious, intelligent, thoroughly trustworthy and can highly recommend his services as an engineer in all branches of internal combustion engine work.

               Yours faithfully,
FERRIERS (NEWCASTLE) LIMITED.

J.N.Ferrier
(Director)

Name C. Ritchie
No. 26   Date 28.9.45

	£	s.	d.
GROSS WAGES	1	2	2
DEDUCTIONS:			
NAT. INS. { H. & P.			
{ UNEM.			1
SPECIAL FUND			
INCOME TAX			
WAGES LESS DEDUCTIONS	1	2	2
INCOME TAX REFUND			
NETT AMOUNT	1	2	2

Open this packet immediately and see that contents agree with above amount. P.W.14

Name C. Ritchie
No. 26   Date 18th May 1951.

	£	s.	d.
GROSS WAGES	6	13	10
NAT. INSURANCE	4	4	
SPECIAL FUND			
INCOME TAX	6		
	7	11	
WAGES LESS DEDUCTIONS			
INCOME TAX REFUND			
NET AMOUNT £	5	2	10

P.W.18

58

Tel. 22663
Extn. 27

D.O.4.

Ministry of Labour
and National Service,
District Office,
17 Eldon Square,
NEWCASTLE UPON TYNE, 1.

Dear Sir,

2 9 AUG

NATIONAL SERVICE ACTS
DEFERMENT OF CALL-UP

With reference to your application for an extension of deferment of call-up to a date beyond the end of your apprenticeship in order that you may take an examination, it has been decided that the deferment already granted to you shall be extended to **31st May, 1951**
_____
(date of last day of examination).

You should inform your employer of this decision in order that he may be aware of your call-up position.

Yours faithfully,

for District Officer.

Colin Ritchie had his National Service deferred until 1951 so that he could complete his apprenticeship with the Ferriers engineering concern. The passage of time (from 1945 to 1951) saw a huge rise in Colin's pay packet although even when serving in the Royal Air Force, he was of course expected to go back into the garage and help out whenever he came home on leave. After doing his basic training near Blackpool, Colin was eventually posted to an RAF radio station at Ballywooden in Northern Ireland. Colin is seen in the centre of the group and still apparently in pyjamas reflecting on the strange working hours required. As the tone of the picture suggests, Colin's National Service was fairly enjoyable and his subsequent love of both soda bread and the Irish people in general was down to his experiences in this period of time. One strange twist of fate involved Colin's requirement to restore six RAF vehicles, which had been mothballed near the station. Once each was made ready for the road, Colin had to drive them to port and take the ferry to Scotland. On one trip, however, he slept in and missed the 'Princess Victoria' ferry but on that trip the ferry sank and had Colin been onboard, he may have lost his life.

Colin Ritchie was to marry Sylvia Robinson on 31st October 1953. They were to have three children – Stuart, Lynn and Alastair – and the picture above was taken just after Lynn was christened in 1956. Stuart (below) soon became aware of the family's involvement in motor vehicles and by 1957, he apparently preferred reading 'The Commercial Motor' rather than children's publications of the time.

Norman Ritchie, his wife Rhoda and daughter Kathleen had this group photograph taken in 1954 when on holiday at Paignton in Devon. Rather strangely, the photographer apparently originated from Darjeeling in India. Although she looks the picture of health, Kathleen wasn't feeling well and the doctor sensed she was catching TB (tuberculosis) and suggested the holiday. Even the trip to Devon was eventful as a detour to see some friends in Hampshire included taking the car to a local garage for a wheel problem. Norman could well have done the repairs himself but not having his work clothes, Rhoda suggested letting someone else do it. However, when the car was jacked up, Kathleen managed to close the car door and knock the car off the jack – fortunately without causing any injury. As the handkerchief across her neck suggests, she herself was badly sunburnt although the subsequent six months she spent in hospital was because of the TB not the sunshine.

Ernest and Mary Ritchie are seen outside the family home of 'Sandylaw' – in Houghton Road – about 1959. Although the week was spent at work, the couple always made time to go to Chapel and both loved to be on the road for their holidays. Even if it just meant an hour or two away on a Sunday afternoon, enjoying the fresh air of places like Rothbury in Northumberland (Mary's home county) always gave them both a lot of pleasure.

WORKS :
OPENSHAW, MANCHESTER, 11
Telephone : EAST 1353
REDDISH, Near STOCKPORT
Telephone : HEATON MOOR 2271

HEAD OFFICE :
OPENSHAW,
MANCHESTER, 11

Inland Telegrams : "GASENGINE" (Phone) Manchester
Foreign Telegrams : " GASENGINE " Manchester
Telephone : EAST 1353 (Five lines)

21st April 19 54

Messrs E & N.Richie,
Engineers,
HETTON-LE-HOLE,
Co.Durham.

TO **CROSSLEY BROTHERS LTD.** DR.

Specialists in Diesel Engines, Gas Engines and Gas Producing Plants. 10720

ORDER No.

Letter 12.3.54 Ref: ER

FORM NO. 750

		£	s	d
To:-	ONE "HH.9" type "Crossley" Diesel Engine No. 145295, complete with Air Receiver, three 3' x 7' Water Tanks, Double Width Pulley and Foundation Bolts.	878	8	0
	Nett....£	878	8	0

Collected by your transport.

Back in June 1934, Ernest and Norman had paid £160 for their first Crossley diesel engine. It gave them 20 years good service but all the Ritchie staff reckoned spending £878-8s on its replacement was value for money - especially because it came with the luxury of an air starter. Although bought in April 1954, the new engine wasn't installed into the plant until August 1955.

silentene
motor oils.

TELEPHONE
HULL 34716

MAJOR & COMPANY LTD.

SCULCOATES

HULL

TELEGRAMS
"MAJOR HULL"

MAJOR & COMPANY LIMITED hereby agree to loan and

Messrs. E. & N. Ritchie, Triumph Garage, Hetton le Hole, Co.Durham
hereby agree to rent ONE FORTY-FIVE GALLON INDOOR OIL CABINET

COMPLETE on the following terms:-

(1)   Payment of 1/0d. per annum rental due on delivery of the
      cabinet.

(2)   Cabinet to be used solely on Oil sold by Major & Company,
      Limited.

(3)   The cabinet to remain Major & Company's property until 500
      gallons of Oil have been delivered by Major & Company Limited
      into the cabinet.

(4)   When 500 gallons have been delivered by Major & Company
      Limited into the cabinet it will become the property of
            E. & N. Ritchie   and this Agreement will be
      automatically cancelled.

(5)   If E. & N. Ritchie   ceases to purchase Major &
      Company's Oil or puts other Companies Oils into the cabinet
      this Agreement will be cancelled and Major & Company Limited
      will have the right to collect the cabinet without repayment
      of the 1/0d. rental.

            ppro E. & N. Ritchie:
Signed   E. Ritchie

Date   Oct 6th 1955.

Signed   Crouchill C
            (for MAJOR & COMPANY LIMITED)

Date   Oct 6/55

Many Hetton folk who knew Colin Ritchie in the 1950s will obviously picture him in this mode of appearance wearing overalls. The Thornycroft petrol engine behind him was recalled as having an autovac system in the fuel line. This worked the same way a petrol pump would work and sucked up fuel from the petrol tank before using gravity feed to take the petrol to the carburettor. The autovac was located in the passenger side foot well but drivers had to remember to switch off the stopcock on a night. If they didn't, all the fuel would run down and overflow the carburettor. They would also have to prime the autovac full again – in the morning – before they could start the engine. LPT 461 – and the Maudslay FUP 187 – were the only two Ritchie vehicles which were almost Nationalised. Under order no. 12/646 made on 27.11.51, these two vehicles should have passed to British Road Services. But, due to a change of Government, the compulsory purchase never went through.

99 DPT was Ritchies first TS3 powered Commer fitted with the one-piece windscreen when it came new on 15th May 1959. Supplied through Northern Autoport, it had a taxation weight of 3 tons 19cwt. With chassis no. CDY 715, it came with a 6 cubic yard body. Long serving Ritchie man Wilson Whitfield shares the photograph.

It seems strange that while Ernest Ritchie was a very keen photographer and took lots of photographs whenever the Ritchie family were away on holiday, it was down to his son Colin to make these first colour records of the Ritchie fleet. It should be noticed that pride of place in any line up saw the company's 1939 Thornycroft take the number 1 slot. In 1960 it was still carrying its horse/bull box and it was used in this fashion until 1963.

By 1964, the '39 Thornycroft had lost its cattle box but was still actively involved. Being used for the coal delivery round, it was re-painted in the colours of Hetton Sand & Gravel and worked until December 1966 before being (partially) retired. Almost all of the fleet are present and lined up in the bottom paddock which is now occupied by Stuart and Carol Ritchie's bungalow. Those figures in the line up that are recognised are: Charlie Wardle, Wilson Whitfield, George Williams, Mathew Hall, Victor Last, Joe Smithson, Dick Hodgson, Larry Bentley and Joe Henderson.

The Lorry Driver of the Year competition always held it's regional heat on the Team Valley Trading Estate at Gateshead and attracted a huge variety of hauliers from the North East. While Joe Wiseman was a regular at this event, it is Larry Bentley who is pictured in June 1967 with the Commer dropside four-wheeler at the first manoeuvre. While Larry didn't shine in 1967, a year later he was to win his class and qualify for the finals, which were always held at Cranleigh.

Triumph Garage has been a fixture on Station Road at Hetton-le-Hole ever since it was built in 1898. The people who have worked there have changed over the years and there have been some slight cosmetic changes to the exterior. While the main frontage started life as a hardware shop (and eventually ended as a fast fit tyre bay, before being converted into offices) its most productive days were when it was used as a car salesroom. From 1949 to 1950, Ritchies were agents for the sleek looking Jowett Javelin but apparently only a few of these were ever sold. More success followed selling Morris / British Motor Corporation products. And although Ritchies were considered as a very small agency, during the five years from 1968, they were selling about 30-40 new cars a year and a similar number of second hand ones. While in 1972 – when the BMC franchise was taken away from them – 47 new cars were sold plus 44 second hand ones.

WUP 555F was Ritchie's first AEC with Ergomatic cab when it came new into service during November 1967. And it was to be the last Ritchie vehicle when gold leaf was used in its livery. Pictured with a high load of Hill's doors, it shares the photograph with driver Cyril Charlton. When Cyril eventually left Ritchies, it was to take up bus driving for the SDO – Sunderland & District Omnibus Co.

It was always a memorable occasion when a brand new motor came into the Ritchie yard and October 1969 saw the delivery of the well liked AEC Mercury GPT 70H. Recalled as being a lovely vehicle to drive that was both fast and quiet, it had a strange demise. It was apparently being shunted on a tow bar (while suffering from an engine problem) and the bar slipped and caused more damage to the engine & radiator. Rather than repair the then ageing motor, it was simply scraped and the chassis rails from this AEC are now in use as part of the garage's steam cleaning ramp. The trio of garage staff in the picture are – left to right – the versatile plant operator Colin Willey, foreman mechanic George Williams and John Dowson, the apprentice.

The AEC Marshal KUP 8J was driven by Jeff Sulkiewicz for most of its working life and is recalled as being a lovely wagon to drive. It looks slightly raised at the front because Ritchies fitted smaller 9.00x20 tyres at the rear to keep the vehicle's height down because of its regular high loading of doors. The body on this 6x2 rigid was made by Jakey Robson of Blackhill near Consett and sports cut outs – round the rear wheel arches – again to keep the running height down.

Ritchies bought two new Smiths excavators. While both could operate as face shovels, the Super 10 was generally used as a drag line to remove the over burden – the top layering of soil, clay and sand - to get access to the gravel. Both of these were sold in March 1972 when the S&G activities were finished. While the Super 10 came fitted with the Gardner 3LW engine, Colin Ritchie was concerned because the Smith 8 was fitted with an Armstrong Siddeley engine. However that concern was misplaced and the engine apparently ran faultlessly for all its time at Ritchies.

The retirement of Ernest and Norman Ritchie in the early 1970s coincided with the closure of the Hetton Sand & Gravel activities. While this photograph (left) of the main crushing plant seems to portray just a mass of crumbling metal, it's very much a reminder of almost 40 years of thriving activity.

Like many of the staff in Ritchie employ, Wilson Whitfield was always considered more like a friend of the family. So it was not unusual for him to share the cab of his Caterpillar D4 with the six-year-old Alastair Ritchie. Seen at Ritchie's Fallowfield site, this was land owned by the National Coal Board but farmed by tenant Joe Nicholson. When Ritchies sold off the D4 crawler in the early '70s, Jim Wakefield bought it.

The Houghton Feast is an annual celebration held every October. It recalls the activities of the late Bernard Gilpin who did so much to put Houghton-le-Spring on the map. The first time E&N Ritchie provided a vintage vehicle to be used as a float (to carry this MGB on behalf of Houghton Motor Club) was in 1970. Of course their '39 Thornycroft was wheeled out of the shed and apart from a lick of paint, it didn't require much doing prior to its first outing on the preservation circuit. Since then, the Thornycroft has hardly missed a season and it's always proved a family favourite. Alastair – seen behind the wheel as a 10 year old – still reckons it's a great vehicle to drive and even Stuart & Carol's son David gave it the thumbs up when he was only 3 years old and about to enter his first Tyne-Tees Run in 1995. In its first 10 years of long distance work, the Thornycroft covered 253,000 miles although it went on to top 315,000 miles by 1966. The Gardner engine was governed to a maximum road speed of 30mph although it returns 25mpg.

Ritchie's first artic was this Leyland Marathon pictured newly painted in May 1975. Bought with a price tag of £11,700 (which included two semi-trailers) the 32 ton gross Marathon is recalled as being something of a Jekyll and Hyde vehicle by both its owner and by its first regular driver Malcolm 'Tucker' Carr. Even before it was painted, the brand new tractor unit caught fire due to an electrical fault and had to be towed back to the supplying dealers for repairs.

Ernest and Norman Ritchie apparently bought their first Dennis about 1937 but it was that bad, they kept it only for a couple of weeks before selling it on. They vowed never to buy another Dennis again and that promise was kept for more than 50 years. By 1989, this Dennis Dominant had spent 14 years working for the National Coal Board and bought for £900, it was reckoned to be quiet a bargain. Powered by the Perkins 6.354 111bhp engine, it returned about 7mpg on local door-to-door deliveries. Built to an NCB specification, the only problem was that the hopper was a single compartment and could only carry one grade of coal.

When your history stretches back more than 100 years, there's going to be some incidents recalled which are particularly disturbing. On 11th June 1985, this was the scene when an unknown arsonist struck at the Ritchie depot. The building involved was the old Ritchie stables which had been rented out to the Summit tyre concern. The yellow Transit in shot actually belonged to the Summit concern that specialised in fitting caps to worn tyres. Although firemen had pushed the Transit out of the stables, the rear of the van was badly scorched and it was written off. There were no personal injuries in this incident.

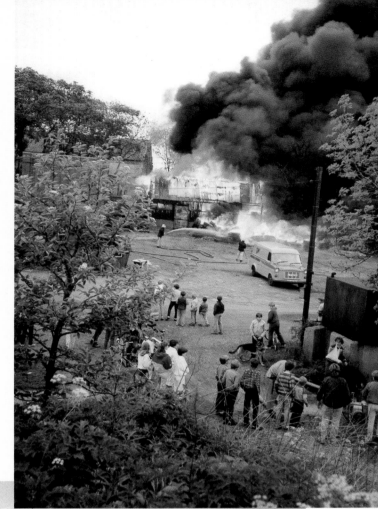

Bought second hand when about 18 months old, this 1985 Leyland Freighter 1114 was to be the last motor which Alastair Ritchie drove before taking up his management desk job. It was bought with a box van body but Ritchies replaced the box with this flat built in house. On the recommendation of John Smiles, the vehicle was sent to McCooms Coachworks in Lincolnshire for the sleeper cab to be fitted. Alastair recalls the Leyland as being a nice vehicle to drive while Ken Leo – the traffic dispatcher at Hills Doors – ensured it was given plenty work. It stayed at work at Hetton for about 10 years.

In the late 1980s / early '90s, this brown and cream corporate contract livery of the Hills Doors operation was used on most of the Ritchie fleet. F794 LTY came new in late '88 and was driven first by Jeff Sulkiewicz. With Cummins 290bhp 10-litre engine and Twin Splitter gearbox, this was Ritchie's first ERF 'E' Series fitted with the plastic bumper. With fresh curtains, the 1975 Crane Fruehauf semi-trailer sports Wilson bodywork. The trailer started life being pulled by Ritchie's first Leyland Marathon and is still in Company ownership albeit for internal use only.

While many of the Ritchie garage staff joined the company at an early age to get some good experience – before moving on to see more of the world – foreman mechanic Frank Wright did almost the opposite. He had worked all round the world but was to end his working days at Ritchies. Recalled as being a gentleman who never seemed to get worried about anything, he was also a brilliant, tip-top mechanic. He is seen relining the brakes on this ex DFDS tractor unit - M618 MEE - that came with air suspension.

Both these tractor units were bought brand new and both share the same contract livery but that's about the only two things they have in common. The ERF EC10 has covered almost 1 million kilometres of virtually trouble free motoring since coming into service during 1997. It's actually just been re-painted (in Ritchie's traditional green livery) but its condition is a tribute to the steady driving technique of Jeff Sulkiewicz. In contrast, the Seddon Atkinson Strato – pictured at Keighley – had a number of drivers yet none of them seemed to be happy with the tractor. Ritchies actually went to the Oldham factory to see the tractor unit being built and it was sold to them by salesman Kevin Openshaw of North East Truck & Van. Prior to working there, Kevin had sold Ritchies ERFs. Powered by the Cummins 14 litre 380bhp engine, it was operated for about six years before being sold on. The name 'Benedict' on the Strato's front grille is the Christian name of the son of Peter Koffman – the BHK owner.

We don't get the snow fall and harsh winters that we used to but there are no complaints from Ritchies about that. Such a view of the yard in March 2004 may make a great photograph but everyone was pleased that the heavy fall was on a Friday night. With the motors normally all being parked up before they started up again on Sunday / Monday, it allowed the snow to melt before there was any panic of how they'd get out the yard.

Bought through MAN Tyne-Tees when it was only about 18 months old, this 1999 MAN 8.165 7.5 tonner has given very impressive service. Used on all manner of local and national express work it was painted by Steve Rennison of RCC Coachworks.

The original Cumbrian registration is something of a giveaway that S548 RAO started life in 1998 with Eddie Stobart. Bought as one of three similar 4x2 tractor units (when about three years old) it's pictured in 2005 when it moved this 1967 Coles crane from Sheffield to Stillington near York. Of particular note with the crane (which was of course built in Sunderland) is that it had the same sort of AEC 505 engine, which Ritchies used in their '60s AEC Marshals. The 1983 Craven Tasker low loader has a 30-ton capacity and with a knock out front end has proved a solid, versatile semi-trailer for Ritchies.

Diversifying into contract hire services saw Ritchies invest in a number of vehicles particularly for this purpose. The MAN LE.150 is on three-year contract with Corus.

The 1925 Morris Commercial T type was bought from Jack Charlton in 1998 when E&N Ritchie were celebrating their centenary. Although already in restored condition, extra work was done to bring it up to concours condition. The vehicle is particularly poignant to the current Ritchie family as it's a solid reminder of the company's operation of similar styled vehicles during the 1920s.

The steam powered 1930 Foden C type RY 9259 started life with FH Richardson of Leicestershire and originally operated as an artic – or flexible six wheeler as Foden preferred to call it. On retirement, it remained in a number of scrap yards – in different parts of the country – but once Harry Wakefield bought it from a yard at Selby in 1971, it was eventually fully restored. It passed to E&N Ritchie in 2003 and has been shown in all parts of the UK and across in Southern Ireland. And its presence has also been requested in Scandinavia for a special event during 2005.

The Scammell model 20LA registered DYS 319 (with chassis no. 6119 and Gardner 6LW engine) was delivered new to Isaac Barrie in Glasgow on 15th October 1945. It worked on the banks of the River Clyde for most of its life with Barrie (and thus the reason for its current name) but was then sold to Sandie Steel of Fife. Sandie used it to haul his own steam engine to events but after the Scammell was badly damaged by fire, it was bought by Frank & Vin Allen. A complete restoration of the vehicle was undertaken by Vin – and Ivor Stafford – and it was purchased by Ritchies on 20th May 2002.

Having operated so many examples of the Ergomatic Cab AEC during the 1960s and '70s, it's not surprising that Stuart Ritchie wanted to have such a vehicle in his preserved collection. WHK 926L is a 1972 AEC Mandator type 2TG 4R – chassis number 22580 – and was new to Dockland Construction of Barking in Essex. It spent all its working life with this company but when sold into preservation it had several owners – without being restored. Ritchies bought it in 1998 from Granville Mason and a full restoration was carried out in the company's workshops. It's been coupled to a variety of trailers although the Castrol tanker in shot is one owned by Iain Wilkinson. With AV760 engine and six-speed (Thornycroft) gearbox, the Mandator is a particularly impressive performer.

The trio of MAN F2000 6x2 44 tonners which E&N Ritchie bought (ex James Irlam & Sons) have proved to be both versatile and excellent workhorses. V86 DNA is pictured leaving the BHK factory at Peterlee with driver Alan Hodgson loaded with two drops in Cornwall. Ritchie Fleet Engineer Steve Cairns photographed Malcolm Carr's outfit loaded with a 17 tonnes JCB machine (of Newcastle Mining Ltd) scheduled for delivery into the Newcastle area.

The marque of Commer was to generally give Ritchies very good long service and while most of them were bought new, XTN 477 was almost three years old when it was bought in December 1958. Chassis no. 81 AO590 was originally new to Blythes Bricks of Birtley and while it was fitted with Telehoist tipping gear, it was ran in E&N Ritchie colours (rather than Hetton Sand & Gravel) on 'A' licence. Driver Alan Harding was a long distance man and his motor did work through Durham Brick & Tile as well as carrying specialist yellow sand.

Foreman George Williams is stood with the long distance flat motor 86 JPT that Alec Howie normally drove. South bound traffic often took Ritchie motors into London and back loads to the North East were often sourced though J&H Transport Services of Peckham. New on 23rd June 1960, the long wheelbase two stroke powered 7 tonner had chassis no. CDY 762-T99Y 9811.

Wilson Whitfield is seen with 321 JPT, which was known as a three quarter length tipper. Having a wheelbase of 11'9" gave the vehicle more operational flexibility in that it could carry cargo in bulk or general haulage loads. New in June 1960 (although it wasn't registered until 20th September 1960) the TS3 diesel powered Commer was chassis no. CDY 741 T82Y 9329. Fitted with 9.00x20 12 ply tyres, it came with a five-speed gearbox. Not all the Commers were geared for the same speed and the garage staff reckoned the ones which could travel the slowest, seemed to stand up better than the quickies.

CHAPTER 7

Like Father, Like Sons

Colin Ritchie and Sylvia Robinson were married on 31st October 1953 and were to have three children – Stuart, Lynn and Alastair. All three were given the opportunity to come into the family business and while sister Lynn only worked on the petrol pumps for a few months, it's perhaps not surprising that brothers Stuart and Alastair were to eventually follow in their father's footsteps.

During the 1960s, those footsteps were to be fast moving as Ronnie Kirtley recalls: 'Although both his Dad and his Uncle came into work every day, they were obviously fairly old men at the time and it was Colin who seemed to run the day to day operation of the business. And when I was there, it was a really busy time as Ritchies were involved in all manner of things.' In fact Norman Ritchie was diagnosed with prostate cancer in October 1966 while Ernest was ill before this.

VERSATLITY

Ronnie started at Ritchies straight from school at the age of 15 just after Christmas 1959. His brother-in-law, the late Wilson Whitfield (a long time stalwart at Ritchies) had got him the job and like most new, young starters at Ritchies, Ronnie's first job was to serve petrol and do tyre repairs: 'I think my first week's take home pay was £2-2s-3d,' recalls Ronnie. By his 16th birthday, he'd moved into the garage as a trainee mechanic and there joined an established team: 'George Williams was the garage

foreman with Jimmy Stoker and Derek Carter being senior mechanics. I well recall Jimmy as he used to love fig rolls and he'd often just buy half a pound of these biscuits from Fisher's Travelling Shop – when it called - and that's all he'd have for his lunch time bait.'

The other mechanic then at Ritchies was Victor Last (also known as Albert, after his father who was a friend of the Ritchie family) who was just out of his training as it was company policy, to always have at least one new mechanic in an apprenticeship. Victor had always fancied being an electrician with the National Coal Board but living at 6, Bleach Green - directly opposite the Ritchie yard - he'd always been

The Ritchie vehicles may have been worked hard but they certainly received a very good preparation before going onto the road. Last application to the cab paintwork was always a coat of Valspar varnish made by the Goodlass Wall concern. 99 DPT is

mesmerised as a child with the rotating drum of the Hetton Sand & Gravel plant.

Victor's first impressions of Norman Ritchie were how clever a man he was: 'He was very good at being able to teach you little things like soldering,' said Victor. Selling new Morris cars (and vans) was something else that Victor recalled Norman was very good at: 'Mr Norman would often sell more new cars than he could actually get from the Sunderland main agents of Turvey. I recall doing six, PDIs in one week, we could be that busy.'

The PDI – pre delivery inspection – could be something of a routine after the new car had been cleaned of the protective wax cover which had been applied in the factory: 'I think we used paraffin to clean this wax off,' said Victor. However, Victor recalled one PDI that was different to many: 'It was a van which Tom Reynoldson – a local painter & decorator – had ordered but something about the engine didn't seem right but I couldn't work out why it wasn't firing properly.'

A trick of the trade is to use a welding rod to check when number one piston was at top dead centre. This idea came to the rescue as when he removed the spark plug and inserted the rod, it almost dropped into the sump: 'Somehow the engine had been

being given the attention before Harry Evans became its regular driver. Harry was a keen campanologist (bell ringer) while short wheelbase Commer men will recall that these motors had their batteries located inside the chassis.

built without a piston and con rod in the number one cylinder,' said Victor. 'I'd never encountered anything like that before – or since – so obviously the van was sent back to Turveys.'

Serving your time at Ritchies meant you had to be versatile: 'The firm had loads of contracts with other businesses to look after their vehicles and these included people with mobile shops and even farm machinery,' says Ronnie Kirtley. 'I suppose at the time, Ritchies was the biggest – and busiest – garage in Hetton. And that's not taking into consideration things like Hetton Sand & Gravel plus the long and short distance motors of Ritchies.'

Looking after the day-to-day operation of virtually everything was Colin Ritchie: 'He oversaw the garage and while Ernest and Norman generally did the car sales, if they weren't available, Colin would deal with folk as we sold a lot of new and second hand cars. Colin also looked after the stores and sold spares, the sand & gravel operation as well as getting loads for the flat wagons – he'd even serve petrol if there was no one around. He just seemed to do every aspect of the business – he was like a dynamo. He even had time to fit the new central heating system for the garage and office.'

Colin and good mate Trevor Dagg (a very versatile naval engineer by trade) fitted the Robin Hood General Boiler and something like 20 radiators around the garage. No big deal you might think, but the Ritchie Thermo Siphon system operated without the aid of a pump and the precision build – and attention to pipe diameter detail – meant the hot water circulated around the system to precisely where it was needed. All the coke boiler required was to be cleaned out on a morning and then banked up on a night, before everyone went home.

ENGINES

Working a 44-hour, six-day week (which was eventually dropped to 40 hours later in the '60s) the mechanic's day generally started at 7.30am. And just like in the earlier days of Jack Delap, first job was to make

Matty Hall is pictured beside 8730 PT, which Jimmy Howlett used to regularly drive. New on 8th February 1962, the Commer – chassis no. CDY 762 3118 - had a Unipower six-wheeled conversion done to it. With a Joseph Bailey body, the vehicle weighed off at 5 tons 2cwt and was fitted with 9.00x20 Michelin tyres. With a rather low 7.4:1 rear axle ratio, the Commer had a five speed, overdrive top gearbox. These early six wheelers suffered from poor brakes because Commer first fitted the same master cylinder as on a standard four-wheeler. Having an extra axle often stretched the capability of the air over hydraulic brakes (especially if they were out of adjustment) although George Williams recalled solving the problem by fitting a second master cylinder to work in tandem with the original one.

sure the Crossley engine which powered the Hetton S&G plant was running. However, in the mid '50s, the original Crossley engine (which was then about 20 years old) was replaced with a similar Crossley made static engine, that had the luxury of being fitted with a starter which operated on compressed air: 'It was normally a simple matter to raise the decompression lever and then use the stored compressed air to turn the engine over,' recalls Ronnie Kirtley. 'Once the decompression lever was engaged, then the engine normally fired - but if you ran out of compressed air, then we had a little trick we would use.'

Many folk who use outboard motors and the like can picture wrapping a length of rope round the starter ring flywheel and

spinning that flywheel (to cough the engine into life) by pulling on the rope. The Ritchie adoption of that principle saw a huge rope wrapped many times round the Crossley flywheel and the end attached to the company Landrover: 'You had to make sure the yard gates were open so you could drive the rope pulling Landrover straight through, but that trick normally worked.'

Other engines in the yard were changing as Ritchie's long-term love of petrol was being phased out in favour of diesel. With Commer still being the cheap and cheerful choice for new vehicles, the Commer diesel engine meant the TS3 two stroke: 'The TS3 needed to be driven really hard,' recalls Ronnie, 'and if you were ever following one up a hill, a good hard driver would get it to de-coke itself by scavenging out the build up in the exhaust manifold. You could see the bits being blown out.'

To those not in the know, these Commer two stroke exhaust pipes looked as though they were on fire, as the red-hot bits of clinker were spewed onto the road. But not every Ritchie driver could manage to cleanse their engine in such a fashion: 'Alan Harding really used to boot his engine hard but Harry Evans – who always wore his old Army beret recalling his days in the Artillery – never went much over 30mph and drove gently in comparison. His motor was always in need of a de-coke as the power output used to drop away.'

To the mechanics at Ritchies, such a procedure was straightforward, if slightly brutal: 'We'd take the TS3 exhaust manifold off and by using a bent metal scraper cum screwdriver, you could get right down into the exhaust ports and scrape the build up

away. An air line would blow out the residue.'

These two strokes could also prove difficult to start on a morning: 'They had very small pistons,' says Ronnie, 'with something called a flame ring fitted towards the top. If that wore, the compression level dropped away and they didn't want to start. At Ritchies, the vehicles were always garaged every night so it meant all the mechanics were involved in having to push the motors out of the garage before they could be tow started.'

The quirk of the Commer de-coking itself – while in motion – was really only cured when Ritchies changed from Mobil Delvac and began using Shell Rotella T engine oil: 'I think Shell must have made that oil specifically for the two strokes,' said Stuart Ritchie, 'as it made a huge difference.' Generally there wasn't much of a problem if the sparks flew, but Ritchies can recall one

939 LUP sports Commer's new look cab and came into service at Ritchies on 8th October 1963. Supplied by Northern Autoport, chassis no. 01374 was a model CBEW 887. Colin Ritchie collected this vehicle when new from the factory at Dunstable although detoured to see his favourite stock car racing – at Newton Aycliffe – on the return trip home. Fitted with Michelin X tyres and a Bailey body, its unladen weight was close to 4 tons 7cwt. Mechanic Roy Todd is seen with the vehicle, which Alec Howie normally drove. Although rated as an 8 tonner, the Commer could handle 10-ton loads quite easily and was recalled as being a nice motor to drive.

By 1964, HBB 578 had passed its 25th birthday and was starting to tire. It was still expected to earn its keep and it was to end its days on the local coal round. The figure in shot is Charlie Wardell and while he didn't drive at Ritchies, he was to spend 6-8 years either operating the sand & gravel plant or as second man on the coal round.

day where such a decoking nearly burnt the garage down: 'Our six wheeled rigid had been out all day and it was garaged as normal on a night,' recalled Stuart. 'What we didn't know was that some clinkers had fallen into the rear mounted spare wheel carrier that also contained odd bits of rope, sheet and chocks. During the night, the embers took a hold with these other materials but fortunately someone saw the smoke and called the fire brigade. The Commer needed a new body but it could have been a lot more serious – and all because these two strokes could de-coke themselves.'

Ronnie recalls a huge amount of camaraderie at Ritchies amongst the staff but of course, there was also time to fool around: 'We used to play jokes on each other and I can recall one day someone tied a kipper to the exhaust of Benny Bowater's motor and of course it stunk. As a pay back, Benny got a trolley jack and raised the rear axle on Lance Howlett's car a fraction off the ground. When Lance got in and engaged a gear, the wheels just went round and he couldn't understand why he wasn't moving. He was told the transmission had gone so

he asked someone for a lift home and just left his car up in the air.'

There was no fooling when it came to fitting tyres as Victor Last recalls the competition as to who could be the fastest to fit four new Michelin tyres onto a car: 'The very supple Michelin walls meant you could almost slip them on by hand and I reckon I was the quickest at Ritchies – although I doubt if my mates would agree.'

One thing everyone agreed on was to help out in adversity: 'I'd saved up £40 to buy my mate's second hand Ford Consul,' recalled Ronnie Kirtley, 'but when I walked out of Barclays Bank in Hetton with the withdrawn cash, a gust of wind blew all the money out of my hand – I was absolutely gob smacked.' Ronnie rushed around but only managed to find two £5 notes but when he ran back to the garage, his mates came back to search and found another £25 in notes. 'The lads said I should report the missing fiver to the police and when I rang in, someone had actually found it – and handed it into the police. I was over the moon to get all the money back.'

A BIT OF CLASS

Working in the confines of the Commer's fixed cab to repair the strange, under-floor opposed piston, two stroke engine became easy – with practice. However, when things got hard, Ronnie recalls you could always rely on the Foreman's strong and precise fingers to come to the rescue: 'It could be very hard in judging how to link back the pistons onto the crankshaft but George Williams always managed to do it – first time, with no fuss. I don't know how he could always do it.'

The mechanics lot became slightly easier once Ritchies began buying AECs: 'I always thought the AEC engine was a bit of class,' says Ronnie. 'Compared to the Commer, a bairn of five years old could put an AEC engine back together – they were that simple and straightforward.'

Ritchies were still buying two or three new motors every year and these were predominantly Commers. However, the company's first AEC – a six wheeled Marshal – was to be registered 124 UP when it went on the road on 6th June 1962 although it was collected from the AEC factory at Southall in Middlesex, two months earlier on 19th April. Naturally Colin Ritchie was the guy who was to drive the new six wheeler out of the AEC plant although on that trip to London his seven-year-old son Stuart accompanied him. 'We took the sleeper train from Newcastle down to Kings Cross in London which was an experience in itself,' recalled Stuart. 'And then we took a taxi to the AEC factory but when we got there, we were told our vehicle had just been given to Scottish & Newcastle Breweries so the Marshal they gave us, was actually one originally built for them.'

The only difference with the two vehicles (which were both in cab & chassis form) had been the make of road tyres fitted: 'The S&N motor had Dunlop tyres,' said Stuart, 'and as we always specified Michelins, the Marshal was taken to AEC's rectification shop – just beside the main gates – to have the tyres changed.' Although the UK's motorway network was still in its infancy in 1962, the trip back to Hetton-le-Hole could easily have been done in one day were it not for orders from above: 'My Grandad and his brother had told my Dad to take it easy with the new AEC and he had to take two days for the trip back so we stopped the night at my Aunties in Nottingham.'

PRISON RUN

The new AEC Marshal was to be joined – during the '60s – by another brace of similar six wheeled AEC rigid flats (plus a four wheel Mercury) and as the biggest motors then in service with Ritchies, they had a varied workload. Sub contracting through British Road Services Teesside depot brought regular work. while delivery of Hills Doors was both a long and good earner. Another regular direct job involved the re-cycling of scrap cable.

The various coalmines of the National Coal Board were known to discard a huge amount of various forms of cable. It may have been waste to the NCB but an enterprising businessman spotted that its copper innards were both valuable – and recyclable. The problem was that salvaging the copper was particularly time consuming, until a cost worthy method was envisaged.

Approaching the Heads of various prisons throughout the North of England, the dealer would pay for the prisoners to cut away the huge amount of rubber covering and strip out the precious copper by hand. It was Ritchies who had the job of first collecting this cable from the North East coalmines and taking it wherever required. And this could be as far as Walton Jail in Liverpool.

Although they didn't have a big fleet, Ritchies would often double shift – or double man - their vehicles so a run across the Pennines to Liverpool could often be done during the night. Naturally, if a new motor was around drivers would have liked to take that, but because the 1945 Maudslay body was fitted with drop sides, it was ideal for the job. Even in the late '60s this four-wheeler did regular work and while some other motors were replaced once they got old, there was often a slice of sentiment involved in whether a vehicle would be kept on the company pay roll.

Another strange job of the early '60s was when Ritchies were asked to remove all the sleepers from the two mile stretch of old railway line which ran from Elemore Colliery towards Seaham: 'We converted the Weatherhill loading shovel to become a huge forklift by fixing two large protruding girders to the bucket,' recalled Victor Last. 'It was a fairly easy matter just to dig down into the track ballast with the Weatherhill and dig out a few sleepers at a time. They were piled up ready to be loaded onto the Maudslay.'

The late 1960s however were to see the requirement for goods vehicles to conform to the newly announced Plating & Testing Regulations. This test was to see the demise of many old stagers while it was the passage of time that was also to catch up with many other major parts of the E&N Ritchie business empire.

124 UP was something special when Colin Ritchie – and young son Stuart – collected it from the AEC factory at Southall on 19th April 1962. Being Ritchies first AEC six wheeler, it had an unladen weight of 5 tons 9cwt 3qrs. Sadly, this AEC was prone to be involved in a series of incidents (not really the driver's fault) and in its time had three different cabs. Originally fitted with a Park Royal built split windscreen version, after the first accident the replacement cab was made in Newcastle. However, Ernest Ritchie took one look at it and refused to accept it. The second replacement was a single piece windscreen Park Royal cab, but when that was smashed off near Dumfries (without causing serious injury to the driver) the vehicle was sold to BM Stafford for spares. Mechanic Victor Last (wearing glasses) and driver Larry Bentley are also in shot. Seen in the background is the small white caravan, which belonged to Joe Dowe. He was a sales rep for the Sunderland based Commer dealership Northern Autoport and kept his 'van in the Ritchie yard. He would come to Hetton and stay in the yard as he reckoned that it was better than holidaying anywhere else.

A.E.C. (SALES) LIMITED

SOUTHALL   MIDDLESEX

RECORD OF CHASSIS NO. GM6RHS 323.   REGISTRATION No.

CUSTOMER   E. & N. Ritchie,   DATE   19. 4. 62.
Triumph Garage, Station Road,
Hetton le Hole. Co. Durham.

SALES ORDER No. 17860.   WIDTH 8' 0"   WHEELBASE 17' 5"

ENGINE	Type	AV0470C/5 LX.		BRAKES		
	Number	6725		Type		AIR HYDRAULIC.
FUEL PUMP, Make & Pt. No.		CAV. 560-3726.		Complete Part No.		
	Makers No.					
	Makers Type			Compressor — Make		WETSINGHOUSE.
INJECTORS, Make & Pt. No.		CAV 562-202.			Part No.	5022-659.
	Makers Type					
PISTONS.	Make	WELLWORTHY ALFINZ		Servo — Make		
					Part No.	
SPECIAL FEATURES						
				Reservoir — Make		WESTINGHOUSE
					Part No.	5021-798.
				Vacuum or Pressure Gauge		
PEDAL GEAR. Part No.		C273 D			Part No.	5049-18.
GEAR BOX		Part No.	Serial No.	Vacuum Tank — Part No.		
Main		D197 AX	68	Air Filter/Anti-Freezer		
Auxiliary						
FRONT AXLE				Low Pressure Alarm		5021-790.
First Front		L219 FX	16486	E1		
Second Front				Foot Valve		5006-516.
REAR AXLE				Unloader Valve		5001-190
First Rear		F290 A	10749	SAFETY VALVE.		5012-55
Second Rear		F291 A	10749	Master Cylinder		5054-305.
DIFFERENTIAL : 1st Rear		F1/2287.		BRAKE.		
2nd Rear				Wheel Cylinders		5012-32.
Ratio		6.92		Front N/S		5012-32.
				,, O/S		
				Rear N/S		5012-96.
FLUID FLYWHEEL				,, O/S		
CLUTCH		J173 D		Hand Brake Ribbon		
				,, ,, Rod		G12/0954.
CARDANS				Brake Pedal to		
Engine to Gearbox						
Gearbox to Centre Brg FRONT.		K7/0177				
Centre Brg to Rear Axle Rear		K7/0181		TRAILER BRAKE GEAR		
Between Rear Axles						
Gearbox to Aux. Box						
Aux. Box to Rear Axles				TOWING GEAR		
				SILENCER		T. 136.
RADIATOR				FUEL FILTER		78-1604.
Part No.		N206 F				
FUEL TANK				POWER TAKE-OFF		
Part No.		S295 B				
Capacity		40 GALLS.				

Geoff Milne photographed Larry Bentley while waiting for some action at the 1968 Lorry Driver of the Year competition at Team Valley, Gateshead. The 6x2 Marshal left the AEC factory on 2nd October 1967 and its Bonallack body was fitted by Northern Assemblies Ltd. With an unladen weight of 6 tons 7cwt 2qrs, it was fitted with two 40-gallon fuel tanks.

Whenever it came to service and support vehicles, the Ritchie mechanics usually had to make do with whatever they could lay their hands on. So even though the Morris Minor 1000 van PTY 830G was small and second hand, to the pictured mechanic Mick Young it was all they had. The van ended up suffering badly with internal corrosion although some of the Ritchie staff may well tell you of some of the odd – big – things this small vehicle has towed.

CHAPTER 8

End of an Era

Nothing lasts forever in the mortal world and the end of a Ritchie era occurred in the early part of 1975. Even though there was eight years difference in the ages of the two Ritchie brothers – Ernest and Norman – there was less than three weeks between their two deaths. Ernest died first on 16th January 1975 (at the age of 82) and his younger brother Norman passed away on 2nd February. Both had been diagnosed with Prostate Cancer – in the 1960s – and while Ernest had been too ill to work regularly during the latter part of that decade, his younger brother Norman had continued coming into work until 1971: 'I think my father always enjoyed working too much,' recalled his daughter Kathleen, 'to ever think of retiring any earlier.'

DIVIDING THE BUSINESS

The E&N Ritchie partnership between Ernest and Norman had lasted close on 40 years, although they had in fact been working together for almost 60 years. It had always been Ernest's wish that his son Colin would eventually take over the business and while Norman agreed with such a request, his share of the business would have to be bought out.

Making arrangements for both the transition of the business to Colin Ritchie and for Norman Ritchie to receive payment for his half share would prove to be difficult and time consuming. Intangible items like good will are very hard to put a price on while even straightforward valuations of

property are difficult. While an item may have a replacement value of say £100 (it would cost that amount to pay for a similar item if it was stolen, lost or written off) that same item may only fetch perhaps £50 if it was ever sold on the open market.

However, once the E&N Ritchie business was fully valued, it was simply a matter of dividing that value in half and saying that was the amount due to Norman Ritchie. The problem of getting the cash together was down to Colin Ritchie and the practicalities in making the payments, is reflected in how it took from 1971 until 1975 for this financial transaction to be fully completed.

An early casualty of the E&N business was to see the closure of Hetton Sand & Gravel. It wasn't a case that there was no demand for this line of Ritchie produce in fact it was quite the opposite. Even during the late '60s, the plant was working flat out trying to keep up with customer requirements. Colin Ritchie had fought hard to persuade his Father and Uncle to update, modernise and totally enhance the plant (which was then over 30 years old) but the two family elders didn't wish to do so.

Colin could have done such modernisation once the Ritchie business became his but such a risk would have been beyond all proportion. This was a time when he was looking to find the capital to buy out his Uncle's share, not look at spending money on other parts of the business, which would have liked investment.

DEATH DUTIES

It had been agreed with Norman that Colin Ritchie would make the transitional payments for the business every three months but once that aspect of the financial considerations were cleared, the spectre of death duties then arose. With the death of his father (in early 1975) occurring long within the seven-year window when such duties are liable, the valuers went back into the Ritchie business and left giving Colin another bill, which he had to pay.

Colin Ritchie had never wanted to do anything else but run the E&N Ritchie business ever since he was of an age to appreciate what the family business was all about. The sheer enthusiasm in which he enjoyed working at Ritchies, was seen by all around him and while Ronnie Kirtley recalls him as being something of a dynamo, that brightly burning light dimmed rather when Colin was diagnosed as having Thrombosis in 1972 and he was laid up in bed for a long time.

The first ever family holiday to the Continent saw Colin return with acute pains in his legs after the flight back from Rome. At first this was thought to be just a continuance of his regular back pain, but when the doctor was unable to find a strong pulse in his legs, he was rushed into the Royal Infirmary at Sunderland. It was then down to Colin's wife Sylvia – who came into the office to help out – and guys like Garage Foreman George Williams who took on more than their job description just to keep the business going.

If you thought the problems couldn't get any worse, then think again. As part of the Labour Government's wide reaching shake up of the Road Haulage world (which also saw the introduction of plating & testing of goods vehicles, plus the requirement for drivers to sit HGV driving tests) the Transport Act of 1968 was to herald the implementation of 'O' Operators Licences.

Long established hauliers like E&N Ritchie had spent almost 40 years nurturing the value of their 'A' licences. It was this small piece of paper, which gave them the authority to work in the field of hire and reward transport. The licences were issued to specific vehicles and also stipulated the vehicle's unladen weight. They could of course be transferred – if a new vehicle was bought – or sold and their value was often calculated in the region of £200 per ton (of unladen weight) even before the value of the vehicle they were attached to be taken into consideration.

An own account carrier, who simply carried his own manufactured goods, operated under 'C' licences, but these had little value as the Traffic Commissioners freely issued them. However, with the strict control over the issue of 'A' licences ('B' licences usually had tighter restrictions attached to them) it gave those in the industry some security against competition.

But once the announcement to do away with 'A', 'B' and 'C' licences – in favour of freely available 'O' licences – it gave carte blanche for anyone to compete (and severely undercut) those already in hire and reward transport. It also opened the floodgates to people who wanted to come into transport and at a stroke simply wiped out the value of those 'A' licences of old. True, the Hetton Sand & Gravel vehicles had been operated under 'C' licences, but once again the value of Colin Ritchie's inheritance was under mined. And the chances of him of making a good recovery with general haulage traffic were put under more stress.

MATTY HALL

Another of the company elders who was to step down into retirement (about 1975) was Matty Hall. Sadly Matty's retirement lasted little more than a year before the problems with cancer claimed his life. Although he had trained to be a mechanic, Matty joined E&N Ritchie as a driver at the age of 18 and gave dedicated continuous service right up to his pension age of 65. Although he drove all manner of motors, he's best recalled with the long service he had with the 1945 Maudslay Mogul.

Reckoned to be one of the best ever

The sand & gravel plant was a permanent fixture in the Ritchie yard for about 40 years. A reflection of how it was designed for another era is shown with the Leyland Boxer 1425 NUP 29J. Supplied new on 1st June 1971 by Murray & Charlton of Blaydon (and fitted with a Tel-Lite 8 cubic yard dropside steel body) this 14 tonner was the highest bodied vehicle Ritchies could buy which would still get underneath the plant loading hoppers. The wear and tear on the plant demanded all manner of repairs although one short cut involved using Stuart Ritchie – when still a five year old – to crawl inside the main feed hopper. Stuart's job was to simply hold a spanner on the dozen or so bolt heads – so they could be refitted – and that way the worn rubber guide strips could be replaced fairly quickly. Apparently the size of the access point prevented anyone larger than young Stuart from getting inside.

drivers at Ritchies, Matty is recalled for all manner of things. Stuart Ritchie remembers how if ever he had a breakdown, Matty could ring in and tell the garage staff exactly what spares were required and even the number and type of spanners they should bring with them. Matty seemed to have such a sympathetic ear for his vehicle and even when sleeping (while another driver was at the wheel) he could almost talk in his sleep and tell them they were pushing his little Maudslay too much.

George Williams recalls the day Matty was told to deliver a load of cement to some premises at Newcastle and even though it was an awkward tight entrance, Matty drove his Maudslay in and turned round in the yard prior to unloading. 'Apparently the management came out,' said George, 'and told him that everyone else had unloaded at the gate as they'd said they couldn't get in. Matty had the gift of being able to look at a gap and know – either way – whether it was wide enough for him. And he seemed to know his way right round the country – he was an ideal long distance man.'

His driving ability was put to the test, when the Maudslay's clutch played up: 'We were really too busy to take the Maudslay off the road,' said George, 'but Matty told me not to worry. So rather than spend the time on the repairs, Matty drove his vehicle for the next six months – without the clutch – until things went a bit quieter.'

Matty's brother Dickie was the local butcher at Hetton and with Matty never marrying, he seemed to be dedicated to his life at Ritchies: 'He never took holidays during the busy summer months,' recalled George, 'but instead took the time off over Christmas and New Year when it was quiet. We used to overhaul his Maudslay every year at that time but Matty would even come into work and help out – when he was supposed to be on holiday.'

The Maudslay was actually built strong enough to pull a drawbar trailer (although it never did at Ritchies) although its recalled for its regular feats of strength: 'Our Smith 10 excavator got bogged down in the quarry,' said George, 'and Matty was asked

if he could help out. He just put a strap on and pulled it out so easily, it was just tremendous to see.'

Victor Last remembered the night when a JT Dove, builder's wagon was stuck in the ice and snow almost opposite the Ritchie yard: 'Mr Norman saw this motor unable to get up the climb back onto the main road so he asked Matty Hall to go and rescue him. And of course, Matty drove down the ramp, put a rope on and pulled him out that easily, it made you wonder what the fuss was all about. Matty and his Maudslay were quite a combination.'

RECOVERING LIFE

The Garage Foreman George Williams was another long serving Ritchie man who left in the early 1970s: 'I'd been there for 23 years,' recalled George, 'and while I'd really enjoyed the time and experience, I just fancied a change so I went to Easington Council and stayed there until I retired.' Colin and Sylvia Ritchie presented George with a gold watch to mark his long service with the company (he only had one week of sickness in 23 years) and also the high esteem in which he was regarded.

It became company policy that George would go out and repair any of the Ritchie vehicles – wherever they were: 'Colin told me of being ripped off, big time, by one garage who he'd called out,' said George, 'so we agreed that I'd go out with spares and enough cash to cover any expense.'

George got as far south as Taunton in Somerset: 'Alan Harding rang in and said that his AEC six wheeler had gearbox problems so I went down with a car and fished out the broken selectors. We carried the car piggy back style and drove the AEC back without some of the gears, but it was better than paying for a garage down there.' George was a big fan of the Commer two stroke engine: 'The simple, basic layout of that two stroke engine meant you could repair say half the flame rings and pistons one weekend, put it back on the road and then do the other half of the rebuild next weekend.'

94

George's knowledge of this TS3 engine meant that a driver ringing on from the A1 at Wetherby reporting a severe knocking was simply repaired by George dropping the engine sump – on the roadside - and reaching in to tighten up an errant nut.

The trick of being able to pull the broken part of a half shaft was routine to the genius of George and such a trick was conducted on the roadside at Hexham. Driver of the Ritchie motor at that time was Lawrie Riley: 'Lawrie always had a Dalmatian dog with him and I remember being called up to the top of Loch Lomond when I had to piggy back his broken down motor. While he'd been waiting for me to drive up, Lawrie had booked himself into this posh hotel and said that both he and his dog had enjoyed a bath – at two o'clock in the morning.'

It was company policy that all the drivers would come into work on a Saturday morning to service and wash their motors although George recalled the day Lawrie's dog was in heat: 'We had to lock the Dalmatian inside the company Landrover – which was inside the garage – but even then it was surrounded by other dogs who could sense the smell.' The Dalmatian did however get caught and was to actually give birth to a litter of nine pups in the Commer cab when Lawrie was driving over the Forth Road Bridge.

Compared to the stories at Ritchies, life at Easington Council would never be as hectic for George Williams. And with the arrival of the first artics, things were set to get bigger and longer in the next stretch of the Ritchie story.

In 1975, Stuart Ritchie was obviously a big follower of fashion. Seen about to leave the yard with the Thornycroft to partake in the London to Brighton run, apprentice John McArdle (in centre) and fitter David French decide to keep their distance.

The Ritchie team have never needed much of an excuse to stand and pose against a wagon in the Ritchie yard. Sid Gibbon is seen beside KUP 8J and while he was to do an odd bit of driving for Ritchies in the 1970s, he's still coming into the Ritchie yard – 30 years later – and doing odd jobs. The small pile on the back of the AEC is the flats used on the bottom – or top – of a pile of Hills doors to protect them in transit. The trio (below) underneath the Charold Autobagger is Roy Todd (on the left) with Stuart (centre) and Alastair Ritchie. DPT 977G was new on 1st January 1969 and came with a price tag of £2,867-10s. With an unladen weight of 5 tons, it was originally painted in the livery of Hetton Sand & Gravel. But with the closure of that business, the BMC Laird 1300LR was repainted to E&N Ritchie.

CHAPTER 9

True Grit

Compared to the heady days of the 1960s, the pace of the Ritchie story during the 1970s was a lot more subdued. A big slice of Ritchie income was lost in 1972 when the BMC Leyland Group decided to re-organise the chain of dealers, who sold their new vehicles. The casualties were small offshoots like Ritchies whose services were no longer required and they were taken out of the dealer network.

Things were certainly a lot quieter around the depot once the Hetton Sand & Gravel work finished and the huge, static Crossley engine switched off for the very last time. What was serviceable amongst the equipment was sold off to other users, although it would be the scrap man - Joe van Blezice - who would take the remainder.

During World War II, Joe had fought as a Commando in Yugoslavia but once Tito had taken control of his home country after the War ended, Joe had come to England and made a new life for himself based at nearby Fencehouses. He was recalled as a larger than life character who was as strong as an ox: 'He could carry a large oxygen bottle on his shoulder as easily as you and I would carry an umbrella,' recalled Stuart Ritchie. 'He always ran an old Bedford – which we used to service and repair – but really he could have carried the scrap by himself – he was that strong.'

Joe was certainly astute as even when the small quartet of Muir Hill dumpers were being pensioned off, Joe knew their true value. Smashing open the casing of their sole drive axle, he pointed out the phosphor bronze crown wheel that would fetch a great price.

SHARING THE LOAD

The biggest problem for Colin Ritchie throughout the 1970s (and well into the '80s) was just being able to financially survive. The pressure on cash flow was recalled by Stuart Ritchie: 'The bank was biting at our heels for about 11 years to make sure we cleared our overdraft and at one time, they insisted we banked the revenue from cash sales at the garage at least twice a day.'

On leaving school in 1971, Stuart served an apprenticeship with the Turvey garage in Sunderland although he also had another job: 'You only worked 40 hours at Turveys as an apprentice,' said Stuart, 'so once I got home, my Dad expected me to work on the motors here.' Such an obligation prompted the re-scheduling of his final City & Guilds examination at Gateshead Technical College: 'We had a break down at Edinburgh with an AEC wanting a new water pump,' said Stuart, 'so my Dad rang the College and persuaded them to let me sit the exam by myself when I got back from doing the repair – in fact I was still wearing my dirty overalls.'

Colin is recalled as being quite persuasive when he wanted to be although his two sons didn't take much persuading to come into the business: 'As soon as I was really old enough to understand the financial fix we were in, my Dad made me a partner in the business. I had to put in all my savings (which was quite a lot, about £3,000 at the time) and even when I was left my grandmother's house, when she died, that went into the pot to pay off death duties. In fact, both Alastair and I – and even our Dad – would sometimes work for no pay at all. As long as my Mother had enough to feed us, the money just went back into the business. It was really a hard time for us.'

Younger brother Alastair had also become a partner – about three years later in 1978 – although he did try and break away from working at Ritchies: 'After school, I took a book keeping course,' said Alastair, 'and I actually got a job at Barclays Bank. But that only lasted about three weeks before I came back here to Triumph Garage.'

The Ritchie empire actually shrank even more around 1982 when the local council compulsorily purchased some three acres of their land, but this wasn't the financial life line it could have been: 'If it had been bought for housing then we may have got a good price,' said Stuart, 'but because they only wanted to build playing fields and allotments, we only got a very small price for it. It didn't seem fair as Colin was thinking about building warehouses on it and those plans were just kicked into touch.'

To help in balancing the Ritchie books, Jack Lumley joined the staff: 'He did work for Houghton Council,' said Stuart, 'but he said he didn't want to be involved when they were creating the Tyne & Wear Authority in 1974. I think he was close to retiring age then but he stayed with us for about 11 years as a sort of company accountant and he really helped to save the company.'

HILLS DOORS

Another saviour of the Ritchie existence was the regular work from the Hills Doors

First registered in April 1975, Ritchie's first ever artic was to certainly leave its mark on the memories of many of the company staff. The Leyland Marathon had chassis number T.25 30102 and an unladen weight of 5 tons 16cwt. Plated for 32 tons gross operation it was capable of almost 22 tons of payload. It had a sparkling performance – when it was running – but was also prone to failure.

factory at Stockton on Teesside: 'We always used to have three or four vehicles doing regular work out of BRS Thornaby and it was the transport manager at BRS – Tommy Ford – who suggested we enquire at Hills. I think we then went on to work there for about 30 years in total.'

Hills had their own 10 strong fleet of four-wheelers, which like the Ritchie motors, delivered doors to every conceivable destination throughout the UK. The big difference with the Hill motors was even those bought in the mid 1970s were spec'd as day cabs and the Hill drivers stayed overnight at various digs. The transport manager at Hills – Bob Bowbanks – is recalled as also having a strange quirk over the sheeting of any vehicle which he saw leaving the yard: 'You had to have it properly roped with cross overs at the back and the sheet on the right way so that you could clearly see the Hills name,' said Stuart.

Although hand balling the doors on and off their motors was a lot cleaner and easier work than some jobs the Ritchie drivers had done, that work was made slightly easier by Hills innovative loading tray system: 'We regularly ran a four wheel AEC Mercury to the Hills south west depot at Bridgewater,' said Stuart, 'and that carried one of their full length trays which was fully loaded with doors. It only took minutes to lift the tray on or off by overhead crane and made the turn round very quick.'

Both Stuart and Alastair were to carry out shunting duties – at Hills – as the first artics were brought into Ritchie service in the mid '70s. As a local shunter, an AEC Mandator was bought although the learning curve of an artic's idiosyncrasies for Alastair was particularly sharp: 'I was probably only about 16 at the time,' admits Alastair, 'but as I was reversing around the Hills yard, I somehow managed to knock down an old toilet block. I didn't mean to do it - although I probably saved them a job in having it demolished.'

Like most youngsters who have been around vehicles for all their life, the joy of driving things which were bigger than the norm was often a temptation that couldn't be ignored – even when the law said they shouldn't: 'Even Colin got done for driving under age,' said Stuart about his father, 'when Ralph Bleanch let him drive his wagon at Dunston. As he was only 19, he was disqualified by reason of age and he had his car licence taken away from him for a time.'

MARATHON MEN

Ritchie's first artic was the Leyland Marathon JPT 848N. Bought along with two semi-trailers, the total investment cost the company £11,770: 'I suppose I pushed my Dad into buying a Marathon,' admitted Stuart. 'There were one or two other hauliers round here who had them and they really looked the part. Colin was a keen AEC man but those first Marathons had a

It may have started life on local work for Northern Gas, but this Transit ran countrywide for Ritchies. Pictured with a neat flysheet, similar loads of toilet cubicles took driver Alastair Ritchie anywhere from Wick in Northern Scotland to Lands End in Cornwall. 'We even delivered toilet cubicles to the Aldermaston Research Centre,' recalls Alastair. 'And every time I go into the toilet of the famous Magpie Café in Whitby, I remember delivering the cubicles there.'

fair bit of AEC pedigree to them and they were also built at the AEC plant in Southall. It seemed a far better motor than the much cheaper Ergomatic cab Mandator which was starting to look a bit dated by the mid '70s.'

The first problem for Ritchies was in finding a driver for the new artic, as all the staff then were rigid Class 2 or 3 licence holders. Malcolm 'Tucker' Carr had got his Class 3 (four wheel rigid) licence when working previously for United Carriers at Dragonville, Durham City and started at Ritchies in 1972 driving the AEC Mercury GPT 70H. In his favour he did come from a strong line of wagon drivers: 'My Dad Robert drove for different London companies and my elder brother Thomas was also a driver,' recalled Malcolm. 'I suppose I was driving an 'Andy Cap' Guy Invincible around our local housing estate when I was only 15 and I did have some artic experience early on – before licences were being issued.'

Malcolm was selected to go to the RTITB driver training school at Sunderland and even though the course with a Bedford TK artic was rushed, Malcolm sailed through. The life he was then destined for was both fast and eventful: 'That Marathon was probably the quickest motor I've ever driven,' he said, 'and could reach 80mph if pushed. It was even quicker than the F88 and F89 Volvos that were around – it just blew them off.'

The problem with the new Ritchie Leyland was its questionable reliability, which was apparent from day one: 'I think this was the first brand new motor that none of the family were involved in collecting,' recalled Stuart Ritchie. 'It was delivered to us by Leyland but as it was just stood in the yard – and before it had even been driven – the main electric lead from the battery caught fire. It was found out later that a screw had nipped that main lead, but it had to be towed out of the yard and back to the dealers for repair.'

In service, Malcolm recalls the Marathon's TL12 engine only lasting about 80,000 miles before it required major work: 'I think it was hardly ever out of warranty,' said Malcolm, 'as with every new engine, the warranty would be extended to cover the replacement – and so on.' Stuart recalled the engine fuel pump was also a regular source of failure: 'The local AEC engineer thought the pump was out of line because the interior plates used to shear - and that took some sorting.'

Phone calls about the Marathon failing were regularly made to Hetton although one frightening incident was also witnessed by one of the company's partners. 'I'd just left Birmingham on the M6,' said Malcolm, 'and for some reason the Marathon just took off.' A failure in the fuel pump – again – caused the throttle to jam wide open with the governor having no effect, Malcolm naturally pulled the engine stop but again that had no effect so he simply hung onto the wheel, dodging the cars in front of him and trying to brake, but with no effect.

Stuart Ritchie happened to be going the other way down the motorway and seeing the obvious problem, he stopped on the motorway: 'By this time, Malcolm was on the hard shoulder as fortunately a piston con rod had come through the block and the engine had obviously stopped,' said Stuart. 'While most other guys would have been perhaps bodily sick with the experience, Tucker seemed to take it in his stride. All he said was, as he looked at the pile of oil and debris underneath: "I think it's really had it this time."'

Another tow in job for Tucker and the Marathon but both would live to pull a few more loads – and with a touch of continental experience for one part of the combination.

RPT 499K was about five years old when it was bought from George Vardy in December 1976. The model 64CU 7205 had chassis number 21485 and the Cummins 205 engine. Being Stuart Ritchie's first ever big artic, it is fondly remembered and was apparently nicknamed 'Captain Marvel.' The reason for the endearment was that it sounded – and went – like a rocket ship. 'Purgatory' is one of the other words Stuart used to describe it.

In contrast to the older 1971 model, the recollections of RVH 948T are all very positive. Although it sports a West Yorkshire registration, it was supplied new to Ritchies in April 1979 through Reliance Garages at Brighouse. Chassis no. 39068 had the Cummins 250 engine, which gave a very fast performance. In November 1979, it spent a week at the Jennings Coachbuilders (then based at Crewe) to have the cab extended when the sleeper pod was fitted.

Malcolm Carr (top) and Jeff Sulkiewicz – right – both started driving at Ritchies in 1974. And 31 years later, both are still on the books.

A627 FGR started life with the Post Office – as a box van – but after a fairly minor accident when about 18 months old, it was written off. Ritchies easily restored the vehicle to as good as new and also did the in house conversion to a platform body. The pictured Alastair Ritchie did all manner of work with the Terrier although the combination came to an end when the vehicle was stolen – complete with its load of doors – in London. The Ritchies reckon it'll probably still be earning its keep in some part of Africa.

CHAPTER 10

Being One of the Family

Jeff Sulkiewicz closely followed Malcolm 'Tucker' Carr as a new starter to the Ritchie driving staff about 1974 and 31 years later both are still on the books. Like Malcolm, he too had several jobs before he came to E&N but he's in no doubt why he's stayed so long: 'It isn't like working for a big company,' said Jeff, 'it's more like being one of the family. They don't tell you what to do - it's more a case of them asking you to do it. They've always been a very good firm to work for. We've always had a lot of fun together and in the early days there was never a dull moment.'

As a Class 2 HGV licence holder, Jeff was given the six-wheeled AEC Marshal KUP 8J with Hills Doors being his first port of call for traffic. And while he was self-taught, Jeff soon became an expert in roping and sheeting: 'It was a case of having to be good at the art,' he says, 'because everything here for many years was flat work.'

As well as a huge variety in the destination of the Ritchie loads, the doors themselves varied greatly. The so-called Popular doors were very light and could be stacked at something like 55 doors high. Fire doors were more substantial and the type of security door lined by steel could weigh in at 1cwt a time. To prevent damage to the new doors in transit, spare doors known as Flats were laid on the bottom of the pile – and on the top – so that they could take the pain of being secured by rope & sheet. These Flats were of course recycled with the vehicle's next load.

SLEEPING ON THE JOB

The modern day, 21st century long distance truck driver expects to have all the comforts of home when sleeping in his cab, but his counterpart of the 1970s – especially at Ritchies – wasn't as well looked after. 'I suppose we were paid overnight money,' admitted Jeff, 'and we could perhaps have tried to find some digs but generally speaking, we always slept in our cab. At least you knew your sleeping bag was clean because some of the digs and hostels of the time were a bit questionable.'

No big deal you might think until you learn the Ritchie rigids of this period – and even the company's first two artics – were all day cabs. 'We fitted curtains you could pull round on a night,' said Jeff, 'but our beds were two bits of board. They rested between the door window and the engine hump so you had enough room to fully stretch out along the length of boards.'

Things got a bit tight when Jeff had Stuart Ritchie with him when he was learning to drive: 'He had his head at one end of the boards and I had my head at the other – so we looked at each other's feet,' said Jeff. 'But to tell you the truth, you were that worn out after handballing doors all day, you could have slept on a clothes line.'

Things did get better when the deluxe version of Ritchie sleeper cab evolved: 'I think it was Malcolm Carr who first came up with the idea of using an air bed,' said Jeff. 'You had to blow it up on a night but the early morning routine was simply to pull the plug out as you were waking up and your weight deflated it.'

Perhaps the worst early morning call for Jeff was when both he and Malcolm were staying at the Mass House car park near Birmingham's Bull Ring: 'I'd given Jeff a few bangs on the door,' said Malcolm, 'but there was no sign of movement. I naturally opened his door to see if he was OK, but this caused the board to slip off the window ledge and it was like a burial at sea, as Jeff slid down the board and out the cab.'

No night heaters either in these day cabs of old: 'Some nights it was like sleeping in an ice box,' said Jeff. 'You'd wake up in a morning and the condensation from your breath had frozen onto everything inside like a film of ice – even the interior curtains were almost welded to the glass windows.'

PISTON PROBLEMS

Jeff recalls his AEC Marshal was capable of 60mph: 'It was fairly quick although I did have the odd bit of piston bother at times.' After George Williams had left the garage, breakdowns became the domain of anyone available, although Stuart Ritchie recalls a number of long distance runs to give assistance: 'People reading this might think we were a right set of cowboys, said Stuart, 'but we didn't have breakdowns every day – it's just they're the occasions you easily remember.'

When the much loved Maudslay of Matty Hall passed its sell by date, it became the Ritchie wrecker by adding a concrete ballast block to its back and fitting a pair of General Trade Plates to it. Generally this was just used for tow in jobs but when the Commer 939 LUP left active load carrying service, it had a crane fitted onto its back: 'We had pulled a two wheeled ambulance type of recovery device with our wreckers,' said Stuart, 'but we'd bought this small

crane about 1950 and it had hardly done any work, so it was bolted onto the back of the Commer. It couldn't lift much but I suppose it fulfilled the legal definition of a breakdown truck.'

Ritchies had a variety of vans and garage runabouts although when the breakdown call came in, anything could be pressed into service: 'I think it was Roy Todd who got stopped by the police when he was using one of our vans to tow an AEC Mercury,' said Stuart. 'The Police said you can't tow a truck with a van and all Roy said was - why not? I don't think they could answer that.'

Another day, another van: 'I remember we'd taken an old Morris 1000 van of Hall's Butchers as a trade in and I was forced to use that one day,' said Stuart. 'But it had never been out of Hetton and when I got to Derby, the brakes failed on it. I rang in to Colin but all he said was the Morris 1000 has a very good handbrake – and wasn't I supposed to be the mechanic. He had a persuasive way about him.'

Stuart has travelled as far north as Kingussie (just south of Inverness on the A9) to repair the Ritchie motors but his

most memorable fright was when he was lying on the A34 near Southampton one early January repairing a prop shaft: 'You don't realize what an experience it is to have a gritter come past and throw salt in your face when you're lying on the road and just cannot get out the way.'

Jeff recalls Stuart and Roy Todd replacing a couple of pistons on the road side near Berwick one day but on a similar type of engine repair on the A38 near Burton-on-Trent, the Ritchie team had to rely on the locals: 'Jeff had dropped a valve with the AEC and I just wanted to replace the piston top,' explained Stuart. 'Because the gudgeon pin is such a tight fit, the only way to get it out – without causing any damage - is to heat the aluminium piston top so it'll expand and you can then ease the pin out. I always carried an old cooking pot for a job like this so I asked Jeff if he would knock on the door of a nearby house and see if he could get the pot filled with boiling water – and fortunately he did. It saved the day.'

MARATHON 2

With the arrival of the second Ritchie artic, Jeff was sent to a driving school at Darlington but he was worried about passing the Class 1 artic test: 'After the third day I was all for chucking it in because I couldn't get the hang of reversing,' he said, 'but I came back to the garage and Colin's persuasive chat said I just had to persevere and of course the next day things just clicked.'

The second big Leyland was a Marathon 2 and had the Cummins 250 engine. Being an ex demonstrator of Hargreaves (the company who had taken over the Leyland dealership network in the North East) it came to Ritchie's painted in that dealer's colours. Repainted Ritchie two tone green, it took Jeff all over the UK as back loads became a good earner for the 32 ton gross artics: 'We carried a lot of potatoes back from Scotland, although going to Cowie near Stirling and handballing 2,500 roof

Being the one and only Atkinson Borderer ever to come to Ritchies, it was a case of once driven, never forgotten for the motor nicknamed 'Norman.' In fairness the 1971 Borderer – chassis no. FC 18930 - was about six years old when it was bought from BM English and was only really intended as a stopgap vehicle. However Ritchies always get the best from all their machinery so 'Norman' had to pull its weight. It's seen leaving Albion's Scotstoun Works in Glasgow with Jim Wilkinson's Albion Chieftain on board (and of course the much travelled Ritchie '39 Thornycroft) after celebrating Albion's 80th anniversary.

tiles – at four or five tiles at a time – was not my favourite job.'

Bagged fertiliser out of the Nitram plant of ICI Billingham was also regular traffic and Jeff recalls one such 20 ton load that he'll never forget: 'It was an awful rainy day,' he said, 'but I was only going to this farm near Morpeth. My Marathon was off the road and I was using an old Atkinson Borderer, which we kept as a spare. It had no power steering, I could hardly see out the mirrors and squeezing down this farm lane, I came to a hairpin bend. Of course I ended up with the trailer sliding off the road and almost into an adjacent pond. I trudged up to the farm and rang Colin but all he said was that what could he do about it. He convinced me I could manage so of course the farm lads got the tractor out and we handballed the entire load off in the pouring rain and then towed the Atkinson out. I was absolutely soaked, but neither the motor or the load was damaged.'

To all at Ritchies, this Atkinson was simply called 'Norman.' The vehicle had been bought from BM English as a stop gap tractor unit after two separate accidents, had taken two of the other Ritchie motors temporarily off the road: 'I'd been involved in one of these accidents near Banbury,' admitted Stuart, 'and the Police had told me to stay at a hostel in the town. It was an awful place and in truth I never slept a wink as I never even took my overalls off – you can imagine what it was like. At breakfast, I remember encountering one of the Hostel residents – who seemed quite a character. They called him Norman Atkinson and of course as we were just buying the Atkinson Borderer from English's, the nickname Norman seemed very apt as that too was quite a character.'

All the Ritchie drivers had tales to tell about Norman. Being such a short wheelbase tractor unit, it had this awful habit of bouncing up and down as you tried to pull away: 'No matter how careful you were with the clutch,' said Jeff, 'it still leapt up and down for the first few yards.'

Norman's greatest escape was one icy day on the A689 road at Killhope in Weardale. Driver Mick Wright had collected a full load of cement from the Eastgate works for delivery into Cumbria which meant the awesome climb over Killhope was the most direct route: 'I think Mick was a bit impatient,' said Stuart, 'and decided to try and get over before the gritter came up. But Norman lost its feet on the slippery surface and just began sliding backwards very slowly. It would have been OK but the artic jack-knifed and ended up over the side.'

All the local recovery Scammell succeeded in doing was to bend the Atky's front bumper so the load had to be tran-shipped onto Jeff's Marathon – and it was all hands to the pumps: 'With the wind chill factor, it was absolutely freezing up there,' said Stuart. 'Stephen Hoggarth – a young apprentice at the time – was helping out but it was so cold that his woolly hat actually froze to his head. But of course Norman came through it unscathed and lived to work another day.'

RITCHIES GO CONTINENTAL

Malcolm Carr got a new ERF tractor unit in 1979 to replace his Marathon and first mod for RVH 908T was to send it to Jennings for a sleeper pod to be attached: 'Being so small, it was a bit claustrophobic,' says Tucker Carr, 'but believe me, it was better than sleeping on the boards.'

Collecting the finished truck – at Jennings – had been something of a problem as Ritchies wanted to pick it up on a Sunday morning (when the factory was closed) but Jennings wouldn't release the ERF until they received the cheque: 'Colin had rang the boss at Jennings,' said Stuart Ritchie, 'about the problem of collection and the conversation had drifted onto the first Jennings cab – and body – that we ever bought, our 1945 Maudslay. When Colin told them we still had the vehicle and had plans for its restoration, they must have

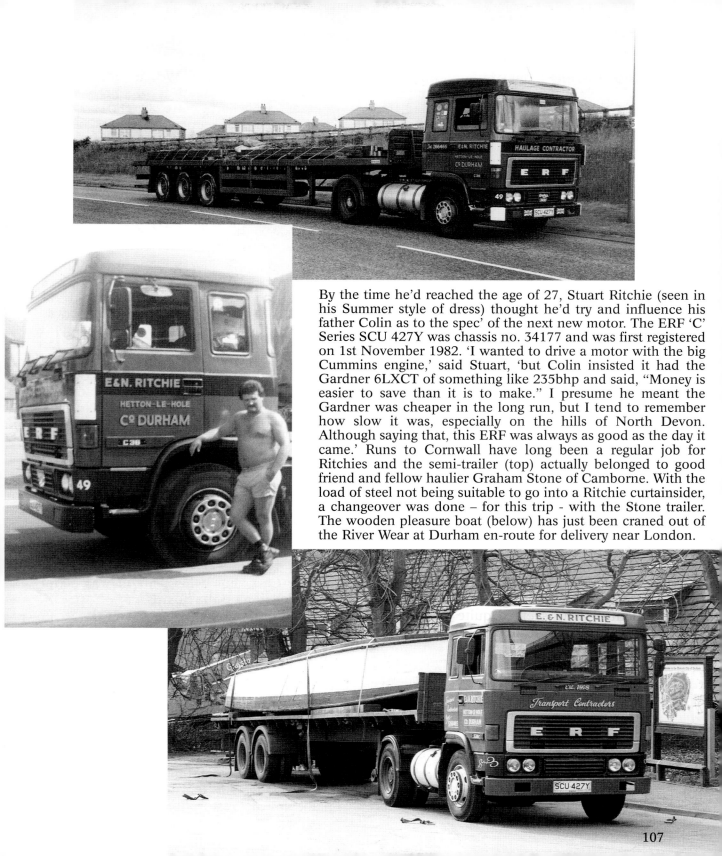

By the time he'd reached the age of 27, Stuart Ritchie (seen in his Summer style of dress) thought he'd try and influence his father Colin as to the spec' of the next new motor. The ERF 'C' Series SCU 427Y was chassis no. 34177 and was first registered on 1st November 1982. 'I wanted to drive a motor with the big Cummins engine,' said Stuart, 'but Colin insisted it had the Gardner 6LXCT of something like 235bhp and said, "Money is easier to save than it is to make." I presume he meant the Gardner was cheaper in the long run, but I tend to remember how slow it was, especially on the hills of North Devon. Although saying that, this ERF was always as good as the day it came.' Runs to Cornwall have long been a regular job for Ritchies and the semi-trailer (top) actually belonged to good friend and fellow haulier Graham Stone of Camborne. With the load of steel not being suitable to go into a Ritchie curtainsider, a changeover was done – for this trip - with the Stone trailer. The wooden pleasure boat (below) has just been craned out of the River Wear at Durham en-route for delivery near London.

Although it sports a Leyland badge, it's recalled that this Chieftain 13 tonner was built mainly with Albion parts - including both its axles. It had started life with the Fisherman's Mutual concern of Eyemouth in Northumberland but once at Ritchies, it had the company's Neville Charold autobagger dropped on its back. The one little quirk it had, was an awful habit of jamming the selectors, which left it between gears.

The first Continental motor to be bought by Ritchies was the Daf 2800 YHN 381Y. The well-known truck salesman Norman Harrison sold it to Ritchies: 'My name's Mr Harrison, 'he always used to say, 'but call me Norman.' The good quality build and the general great performance of this Daf were to be an eye opener for all at Ritchies. It's seen having just left the Tyne Dock with the tipping semi-trailer, which the company ran for a short time in the late 1980s. Like most of the Ritchie vehicles, it underwent a repaint into contract livery.

realised we had something about ourselves and the response was: "We'll trust you – just post the cheque through our letter box when you collect the wagon," and that was it. It made us feel quite good to be thought of in that way.'

A regular contact for Ritchie back loads was Starmile Transport of West Drayton in Middlesex. And it was this company which introduced Malcolm Carr to Continental work. Loads of coconut – through Starmile – from Mars at Slough took Malcolm to the Mars plant in Germany (to make Bounty Bars) while he also recalls taking a load of second hand TK Bedfords to Amsterdam docks: I think they were then shipped out to the Caribbean,' he said.

First trick that Malcolm was taught was how not to get your permit stamped: 'You were limited back then as to the number of times you could take a load onto the Continent. Every load needed a permit but I soon learnt that you somehow had to show the permit – at various border posts and customs points – but you then had to pull it away before it was stamped.' Or as other Continental drivers of the time will know, resort to other tricks to keep that permit valid as long as possible.

Computers from Glasgow were a regular load and one such hurry job meant Malcolm might spend Christmas abroad: 'Honeywell Computers promised that if we could deliver the loads into Northern Italy before Christmas, they would get us home in time for the holiday.'

What they didn't realize was that 'Tucker' – at that time – had a fear of flying: 'We ran back empty to Lyon and they planned to fly me – and another Starmile driver – back to Heathrow,' recalled Malcolm. 'I told them I would never get in a plane so we ended up hiring a Hertz car and driving home. So of course after the festive period, we had to drive back to Lyon to return the hire car, pick up a back load for the motors and then come home.'

Climbing up to the Mont Blanc tunnel was a route that Tucker will never forget but life for this Englishman abroad wasn't too enjoyable: 'I liked the driving but it wasn't much fun spending weekends over there – waiting to tip or to load.'

Back in the UK, the problem for Tucker was getting into the odd scrape or two and he ended up breaking his collarbone – twice. 'I was down in Penzance unloading some doors and the wind blew me off the motor,' recalled Malcolm. 'I was taken to the local hospital and when they realised how far North I lived, they wanted to keep me in. So I told them I could recuperate with an Aunt who lived just down the road. I made that up, so they'd let me out, so I put a pillow on my knee – to support the bad arm - and managed to drive the artic all the way back to Scotch Corner. I was about shattered then so I rang in for someone to come and pick me up.'

The second time he broke his collar bone was at the Isle of Dogs but fortunately Stuart Ritchie was with him in a second artic: 'I went with Tucker in the Ambulance,' said Stuart, 'but even when I was pushing him round in the wheelchair, he was telling me how to drive it.' Piggy backing the two motors was how Stuart brought the two artics back to Hetton: 'Even when we went out on breakdowns with the van, Colin still expected us to save fuel coming home by piggy backing one vehicle on top of another. But on this occasion, I had to persuade a digger driver to build a huge mound of earth so I could drive one motor up it and onto the semi-trailer of the other.'

Yes, when you worked at Ritchies, you had to be versatile: 'Colin always knew what he wanted,' said Stuart about his father, 'and to him there was no such word as impossible.' However, one thing Colin never enjoyed – in his latter years – was the best of health and that was one problem he would never surmount.

Colin Ritchie's love of the Gardner engine was perhaps reflected in the purchase of KYA 861T. Colin – and son Stuart – had gone to Worcester to look at a 7 month old ERF, that was for sale, but it was this ex Wincanton Transport 7 year old unit (that had been stood in the corner of the yard) which became the Ritchie purchase. The reason was this tractor unit had the Gardner 8LXB engine and Colin simply fell in love with it. It proved to be a 'hell of a runner,' and when sold on by Ritchies, it was bought by a showman who stretched it into a four wheel rigid. When the chassis finally ended its days, the Gardner 8LXB was sold for export.

In March 1987, Ritchies joined a franchise agreement with Connect UK whereby they delivered (and collected) across a certain area of the North East. This Leyland / Freight Rover Sherpa van was bought specifically for this contract which lasted two years.

CHAPTER 11

Stability

After the roller coaster ride of happenings through the 1970s, progression of the 1980s saw a gradual stability come to the physical and financial well being of E&N Ritchie. Things weren't all plain sailing, because with Hetton-le-Hole still being a strong coal mining community, the year long Miners strike (from early 1984 into 1985) had a devastating effect on the garage. 'People just stopped buying everything,' recalled Stuart Ritchie. 'Even petrol sales went down never mind things like tyres, spares and servicing – it was just a period of total recession. People round here just didn't have the money.'

Making do and mend has long been a Ritchie philosophy so while the garage went quiet, Colin developed a variety of other work for the haulage vehicles. One very different phase of work - which was started in March 1987 - was with Connect UK. Every morning a semi-trailer loaded with parcels / smalls was brought into the Ritchie yard from Connect's central hub at Nuneaton. Ritchies were responsible for deliveries and collections across the eastern part of County Durham and some parts of south Tyneside.

A Leyland Sherpa van was bought specifically for this job and while it had regular drivers, all and everyone was expected to pitch in at times if there was a driver short. Doing anything up to 40 drops and 25-30 collections in a day wasn't easy – to those who'd never done it before - but the main priority was getting back to the yard before 6pm, so the artic could be loaded for the night time run to Nuneaton. Although fairly lucrative, Colin decided not to renew the franchise contract after it had run for two years. This proved to be of good foresight as Connect were soon to cease trading.

Finding ways of cutting down on costs of your own vehicle repairs was fairly easy for Ritchies: 'Recycling may be in vogue today,' said Stuart, 'but we've been recycling old vehicles for spares and the like for many years. We've always kept a good supply down the field.'

Making things in house is how Ralph Ritchie got things going in the first place. So it'll come as no surprise to learn that his grandson Colin Ritchie was at his happiest when he couldn't get something. He then had the excuse to don his dustcoat and head for the lathe to spend hours making the part in question. Time spent on jobs like this never came into the costing equation – it was simply a labour of love.

Winning one service contract in particular gave Colin a huge amount of satisfaction: 'Colin spent a lot of time preparing the tender to look after the 15 milk floats of Houghton Dairy Farm,' said Stuart. 'Some of these floats were 30 years old but as well as their general servicing, Colin loved it when he was asked to rebuild them. We had something like a production line set up, but stripping down then refurbishing vehicles into good as new condition was right up his street.'

RUN FOR FUN

With Colin being a long term, active member of Houghton District Motor Club, it's perhaps no surprise that as he got older – and left his car rallying days behind – he turned to the heavier commercial

Ritchie's second Daf was to be this 4x2 3300. Bought second hand when about four years old, it was originally operated by Pilkingtons of Chester-le-Street. Again it proved to be a good truck for Ritchies although the original cab was replaced after suffering from corrosion. Friend of the family Vin Allen is seen with the Daf about to head north from the Great Dorset Steam Fair.

B881 EDP proved to be another excellent second hand buy for Ritchies. Powered by the Big Cam 290 Cummins engine, the 6x2 started life with Calor Transport. Being just a day cab unit, it was double shifted a lot of its life carrying paper from Blyth to Manchester and then back loading (with a different sort of paper) from Ellesmere Port to Sunderland.

preservation scene for his motoring enjoyment: 'I think I set things going,' recalled Stuart, 'because when I heard about a steam event at Birtley – in 1970 – which some friends were going to with an old lorry, I suggested to my Dad we should take our old 1939 Thornycroft. We had stopped using it on the road but it was kept as a loading platform – in one of the garages – and it didn't take much to make it roadworthy again.'

The lorry preservation scene may be very strong today, but 35 years ago the only events of note were for steam powered vehicles. So when the Ritchie family took their 32-year-old Thorny to the North of England Steam Traction Society's event at Chester-le-Street in 1971, it was one of only three non-steam powered commercials listed in the programme. Naturally these three vehicles were parked together and alongside the Ritchies was Tom Pearson of Masham, with his 1927 Morris Personnel Carrier.

Tom was a regular on the Show scene so as some encouragement to the new starting Ritchies, he invited them to the following week's steam event at Masham. This was the start of a long friendship between the Pearson and Ritchie families, but of particular significance to Stuart was he'd meet his wife to be – Carol Pickles as she was then – on one of his many trips down to Masham: 'Stuart became good friends with Tom Pearson's son David,' said Carol who was brought up in the nearby village of Grewelthorpe, 'and he ended up spending most of his holidays down there - although with the Pearsons having a farm, they were working holidays.'

Carol was only 12 when she first met Stuart but 12 years later (in 1984) they were married: 'I'd been offered a job in Durham City itself,' she said, 'but Colin said that seeing I was now one of the family, why didn't I come and work in the family business. And to tell you the truth, I really

Bought from auction as a chassis / cab, this Leyland Roadrunner was ran by Ritchies for about three years. When sold on, it was bought by GW Wright, the agricultural merchants of Hetton.

liked being invited in that fashion and I've been working here ever since. Although I don't really look at it as being a job, it's more a part of my life.'

BEST IN SHOW

The Ritchie Thornycroft has been road running ever since that first outing although with a top speed of 30mph, it can be time consuming. When the Ritchies first did the London to Brighton Run, it took them five days to do the round trip to Brighton sea front, as there was no low loader piggy backing to the start off point in those days.

Colin Ritchie was one of the founder members of the Historic Commercial Vehicle Society's North East Region when it was set up in the early 1980s. He was very active with the HCVS although what also became a regular family treat was the annual visits to the Commercial Vehicle Motor

Show: 'Before the show went to the NEC at Birmingham,' said Stuart, 'they were held either at Earles Court in London or Kelvin Hall in Glasgow – the show alternated between the two venues every year.'

Seeing what the latest and greatest had on offer was something of a mixed blessing for Colin as he was an out and out British patriot: 'We bought a Daf in the early '80s,' said Stuart, 'but you wouldn't believe how my Dad argued things, just to justify it was almost a British made wagon – and anyway, the Dutch people were very close kin to the British. It was a laugh but he gave short shrift to the rest of the Continentals and almost hated the French.'

In 1990, Renault had the futuristic Magnum on their Motor Show stand and standing head & shoulders above any other commercial vehicle then on display, it was being feted by one and all – but not Colin Ritchie. 'Renault couldn't make a pedal car,'

113

One of the big lessons Stuart Ritchie learnt from this particular job, was you should never presume anything. Ritchies had been asked to move this fishing boat the short distance from Fence Houses to Penshaw for George Riches of Fence Line Transport in the late 1980s. Even getting it out of the workshop / shed had proved difficult but mechanical means had been provided to load it onto the semi-trailer. It was thus presumed that some sort of lifting device would be provided at the delivery point. However, the only form of lift the boat was to get was when the River Wear floated it off the partially submerged semi-trailer. Although a proper ramp was in situ (generally for the smaller private car & trailer combinations to use) Stuart was concerned about stability so he hooked a chain on from the Daf to a JCB – which is out of shot. Assistance wasn't in fact required and the water didn't cause any damage to the trailer although to discover the second big lesson of this job, you'll have to ask Stuart himself.

was how Colin dismissed the mind blowing Magnum so there wasn't a lot of point in having a chat with the salesmen on that stand.

OUT OF BREATH

The 1990 event was to be the last Commercial show in which Colin, Stuart and Alastair all attended together. Colin's health problems had probably began as a child when he caught Rheumatic Fever, which was discovered – later – to have weakened his whole body. His adult problems became apparent in 1972 when he suffered from Thrombosis after his air flight from Rome. And things got worse after a heart attack in 1978: 'He collapsed at home,' recalled Stuart, 'but fortunately our doctor – Alan Johnson – lived nearby. I remember he ran round in his slippers and organised an ambulance to take Colin straight into hospital. But even after that

trip, I remember how Colin complained about the springing and ride of the Bedford CF chassis which had taken him there.'

After this attack, Colin was warned that he would have to give up smoking – and he did. However, the long term effects of having smoked so many cigarettes, for such a long time, was to take its toll on his heart & lungs.

If will power alone could have kept him going, then Colin Ritchie would still be alive today: 'Even though he smoked very heavily,' said Carol Ritchie, 'when Doctor Johnson said he couldn't afford to smoke again, he stopped just like that. And I never even heard him say that he fancied another cigarette ever again. He could be so very determined when he wanted to be.'

As part of Colin's heart attack treatment, he had to take a blood-thinning drug for the rest of his life. This meant that simply having a tooth out meant a visit to hospital, as it would have been too easy for him to simply bleed to death, at a normal dentist. Colin took his failing health in his stride even though problems kept jumping up and hitting him.

Once Ritchies had stopped selling cars, the showroom was converted to a fast fit tyre shop. It was a routine procedure to put a tyre and wheel onto the machine and let the lever separate the rubber from the steel. But as Colin was passing the machine – in June '87 – he noticed something was wrong and went to reach over to put the tyre right. Sadly the operator didn't see that Colin had put his hand into the machine and the resulting action saw Colin loose two of his finger ends as the lever came down onto his hand.

With blood spurting everywhere, the only one who didn't seem to panic was Colin himself: 'I think the customer nearly fainted,' said Carol, 'and the machine operator was being sick but Colin hardly seemed bothered. He simply organised to have his finger ends picked up; wrapped something round the injury to stem the blood flow, as well as arranging for Wilson Whitfield to take him to hospital. He just took things in his stride and was so matter of fact about the whole incident.'

The two finger ends were sewn back on but within two weeks they had gone gangrenous and they had to be cut off. But even with that operation in Shotley Bridge Hospital, Colin elected to have it done quickly, with just a local anaesthetic – so there'd be little fuss.

Colin was generally a quiet person who rarely raised his voice and never seemed to swear: 'If he did lose his temper,' said Stuart, 'then it was really about something important but "Flippen" seemed to be the strongest swear word he'd ever use.'

The pain he went through for the last 20 years or so of his life must have been severe but he rarely let on. Tucker Carr recalled how he always wore fur-lined boots to try and keep his feet warm, as his blood circulation was that poor. He normally used a pair of polystyrene blocks to rest his feet on – when sitting at his desk – to keep them off the cold floor. Investing in anything more expensive as floor covering was not how Colin Ritchie looked at keeping his business afloat: 'He used to look at the offices of any prospective customer,' said Stuart about his father, 'and say "The deeper the pile of their carpet in the offices – then the less time they will last in business."'

Colin only lasted in the Ritchie business to the age of 61. The last few months of his life were really heavy going but Colin would drag himself into work every day, even though some times he'd just have to sit in the car outside, while he built his strength up to walk indoors. He still retained very tight control of the business reins as he just loved being involved however, the day beckoned when he couldn't find the strength to go on: 'We'd arranged to go down and see John Smiles,' said Stuart, 'who was then working for Ford & Slater at Lincoln.' (This was the same John Smiles who had gone to school with Colin at Hetton and worked as a mechanic at Ritchies. But even when he left Ritchie employ, he was to become – and still is – a firm family friend.) 'We were after a second hand six wheeled rigid for the Hills Doors job and John had something suitable to look at. Colin loved doing trips like that but simply said he couldn't go.'

Taken into hospital, it was diagnosed that he required five bi-passes to his heart. But before the operation could be started, Colin had a heart attack and while the bi-pass operation was carried out, Colin never recovered and died on 2nd November 1990.

To say that the Ritchie family, the Ritchie customer base and a lot of the Hetton locals were devastated, would be putting it mildly. People from as far as London and Cornwall travelled to join the hundreds who tried to get into the Union Street Methodist Church for Colin's funeral service. And even ex employees like Victor Last came back to run the garage business for a few days while the Ritchie family were coming to terms with what had happened. It was the least they felt they could do – Colin had been held in such very high esteem, by so many people.

When a Ritchies' customer asked them to provide a six wheeled rigid, Stuart was to buy this second hand Daf 2100. However, this is probably the only purchase which Colin Ritchie didn't agree on. He thought the intended driver – John Chisholm – wouldn't like what Colin thought was a 'Rabbit Hutch' style of sleeper pod. John actually loved it but sadly Colin didn't live long enough to learn that. The last outing together of Stuart and Colin (left) and Alastair – who is out of shot – had been on 6th October 1990 when they travelled by train to celebrate the centenary of the Forth Rail Bridge. After Colin's sudden death, a fund was set up to help heart patients. Donations were later given both to Hetton Health Centre and the Cardio Thoracic Intensive Care Unit at the Freeman Hospital in Newcastle.

Only a few years separate these two line-ups of the Ritchie vehicles but the appearance couldn't be more different. By the late 1980s (top) the company's standard green livery had almost disappeared. As the demands of dedicated operation required a contract livery, it was only when that work finished could the E&N colours be repainted onto their vehicles. Although Daf had done Ritchies very well, they were never bought strongly. Foden also only had token representation into the Ritchie fleet although their Foden Fleetmaster – EYR 23V – went so well it was known as the 'Mile Muncher.' It was later sold to Van Hee Transport in Newcastle and it ended its days taking the Van Hee trailers for test.

CHAPTER 12

Into the 21st Century

Over the last 15 years, the efforts of the current E&N Ritchie management team have ensured the company is now firmly established on the North Eastern business scene. As well as the garage services of fuel, car & commercial repairs and maintenance, E&N Ritchie's transport operation has grown into double figures. And with the majority of the fleet being 44 tonners, it means Ritchies are moving far more freight now by road than they've ever done.

The company have diversified into van hire and leasing out vehicles to dedicated contract customers, while the building of brand new warehousing on site at Hetton has also allowed packaging services to be on offer. Other diverse services are given to a wide variety of customers which meets the business plan that Stuart Ritchie identified soon after his father died: 'I don't think Colin did it deliberately,' said Stuart, 'but as he had virtually ran the firm – by himself – for almost 30 years, a lot of the business know how was kept in his head. And in truth, it was difficult to just pick up the reins when he died.'

At first, Stuart was to be helped by Wilson Whitfield who had been a close confidant of Colin for the garage's operation, but to enhance their haulage arm, E&N Ritchie were to turn to Marshall Higgins for help: 'Being reliant on Hills Doors for all our work meant we'd almost lost our identity,' said Stuart. 'Most of our vehicles were painted in the customer's colours and I can imagine some people might have thought E&N Ritchie had gone out of haulage, as you hardly ever saw our own liveried vehicles anymore. But when Marshall joined the company, he brought a lot of experience with him – and he probably came just at the right time.'

NEW CHALLENGES

As well as the practical problems created when Colin Ritchie died, there was also a huge amount of emotional distress to the family, which was summed up by Alastair Ritchie: 'I know a lot of families are very close,' said Alastair, 'but as well as working closely together, we also lived and socialised together. And once Colin died, there was a huge hole left behind. It took a lot of coming to terms with but fortunately I met Annette – my wife to be – and she helped me through it.'

As soon as Alastair had became involved as a partner in the business (back in the late 1970s) he joined the driving staff: 'Being only 17 back then meant all I could drive was a Transit pick up,' he said, 'and depending on their weight, I'd sometimes just be carrying 35-40 doors. Although saying that, I could also have 10-15 drops simply because the Transit was more flexible in operation.'

Like the other long distance Ritchie drivers, Alastair quickly learnt how to sleep across the front seats of the Transit and while you might think it's more comfortable in the cab of the subsequent, bigger Leyland Terrier 7.5 tonner, Alastair recalls it was possibly worse: 'The problem was the

Not every visitor centre in England would have welcomed Ritchie's ERF low loader. But when Stuart, Carol and David Ritchie were returning from an event at Cork in Southern Ireland during 1995, they were made more than welcome when they stopped off at the Waterford Crystal premises (top). Rather aptly D52 MKH started life with Rockware Glass but the main attraction to the Irish observers was the 1912 Marshall agricultural engine being carried on the Craven Tasker low loader. Later in its Ritchie life, the ERF was converted (in house at Ritchies, of course) to a rigid curtainsider. With 10-litre 290bhp Cummins engine, the motor spent most of its time in top gear – it had that much power in hand.

Terrier's gear lever,' he said, 'because you couldn't seem to put it in any gear where it wasn't sticking up into your body.'

Although Ritchies were delivering a huge number of doors by artic, there was always work for the smaller rigids (carrying 120-130 doors) albeit at a large number of drops. Alastair often worked the south coast of England – with the deliveries starting at Hastings – but another regular trip into London brought about an unforgettable experience: 'I wasn't far from my regular drop off point,' said Alastair, 'so I stopped outside a paper shop and dashed inside for some bits & pieces. I obviously wasn't quick enough as while I was in, someone stole the Terrier – and all the doors. We never saw the motor or the doors again.'

After the Terrier, Alastair had an 11-ton Freighter, which was sent to the McCombe body building concern in Lincoln to be converted into a sleeper cab. Giving a just in time express service was well appreciated by the Ritchie customer, but that high standard of service didn't prevent them from being a casualty after the customer re-organised their operations: 'Hills had become part of the Crosby Group,' said Stuart, 'and they had manufacturing outlets across the country. It seemed natural they would rationalise their affairs but it hit us really hard when the Stockton work finished altogether in late 1992.'

However as that door closed – literally – the newly arrived Marshall Higgins business development expertise was immediately put to the test: 'Marshall found us some good regular work,' said Stuart, 'and the fact we're still with many of the customers he first introduced us to, lets you know they are happy with the level of service we give them.'

TEAM EFFORT

Being such a relatively small operation, any success achieved by E& N Ritchie has always been down to it being a team effort. Obviously the input into that team varies as to the different roles that are taken and of

One of the problems in operating full size curtain side semi-trailers is they are susceptible to side winds. The strange thing about this incident is it occurred on Christmas Day and Ritchies were actually given advance notice of it happening. A security guard at the premises in Peterlee noticed the empty semi-trailer was starting to move around in the high winds so he decided to ring Alastair Ritchie at home. Alastair asked if the guard could open the curtains (to allow the wind to blow straight through) but just as the instructions were going down the phone line, a stronger gust blew the empty trailer over.

Lonsdale Marine built all manner of vessels at their premises at Easington Lane and Ritchies were favoured hauliers to handle their awkward charges. This 40' cruiser had a Volvo engine and while vessels like these were taken all over the country, this particular one was destined to be craned off into the River Ouse near York.

course, all teams need to have a leader. On paper the affairs of Ritchies are now shared between the three partners of Colin Ritchie's widow Sylvia and her two sons Stuart & Alastair but in practice Sylvia lets her two sons take the strain: 'Our Mam worked her socks off doing all sorts in the business during the 1970s when things were really bad,' the two brothers agree, 'so it's great she can now take things a lot easier.'

Being the eldest, you would think Stuart would take command but again in practice, the make up of Ritchies diverse affairs means the two brothers share the different pressures. With the Ritchie road haulage operations being based at their main customer's factory in Peterlee, Alastair – and Marshall Higgins – look after that side of operations. Stuart, his wife Carol and the Ritchie admin & garage staff work from Hetton although in truth, the area around the coffee machine at HQ is also something of a meeting place for friends, visitors and of course, team members old and new.

That Ritchie team took a severe knock in April 1993 when long serving member Wilson Whitfield had a heart attack: 'I was on the diesel pump filling up,' said Stuart, 'as I had just done a night run somewhere. I heard this bang from up the road and when I looked round the corner of the building I recognized Wilson's car as having crashed into the wall.'

Fortunately there was no one else involved but having that crash had apparently saved Wilson's life: 'Talking to the paramedics later,' said Stuart, 'they explained Wilson's heart had stopped and that's why the car had gone out of control. But the impact of the subsequent crash had actually shocked his heart back into life again.' Wilson would never come back to work again at Ritchies but at least he was to enjoy 11 years in retirement after 40 years service at Ritchies.

THE FUTURE

In a book of this nature it's always easier to write about what has happened in the past – rather than trying to foretell what will happen in the future. While Ralph Ritchie had the original vision of setting up the business, I doubt if he could ever foresee they would move from making mangle rollers to operating a highly popular charabanc service.

It's also hard to believe that while the two brothers – Ernest & Norman – were delivering in their small four wheelers in the 1920s, they would ever dream Ritchies would become so heavily involved in sand & gravel operations. And I doubt even the late Colin Ritchie would ever dream that the Ritchie fleet of motors would be painted silver – instead of their traditional green.

The change of colours is nothing mind shattering, but perhaps an indicator that Ritchies have always had the ability to remain flexible in their approach to their entire business affairs. It's this flexibility that has kept them alive and active over a continuous history, which has seen five generations of the family work through 107 years.

Looking at a chain of this nature suggests there's some pressure on Stuart & Carol's 13 year old son David to eventually take over the reins. Such a suggestion couldn't be further from the truth. It would be great if he kept the story going but in this fickle modern day world of road transport, nothing is ever guaranteed.

But even if the Ritchie story ended tomorrow, the family could look back with great pride on what they've achieved – and there's no great secret to their long life. Working hard and being honest & open to those you're involved with has served them well. It's an attitude which perhaps sends a message to us all.

Pictured in Holland waiting for the North Shields ferry back to Tyneside (above) Ritchie's 3.5 tonne Iveco Daily had just completed an express delivery of laminated foil into Germany close to the Czech border. Blendex Food Ingredients are based at Hetton-le-Hole and are another company who have availed themselves of an E&N Ritchie Contract Hire vehicle. The MAN 7.5 tonner delivers the special Blendex ingredients around all parts of the UK.

A look round the Ritchie operation of 2005 (see above, below and overleaf) sees all manner of activities. Semi-trailers in a customer's dedicated livery can be seen although the latest brand new addition to the Ritchie trailer fleet is a purpose built, King tri-axle step frame of around 35 tonnes payload capacity. Bought primarily to haul heavy-duty plant and equipment, it's easy loading ability – through electrically operated ramps - means it's ideal to handle the Ritchie vintage collection of vehicles.

E. & N. RITCHIE

MOTOR ENGINEERS AND AGENTS
HAULAGE CONTRACTORS

Established 1898

Triumph Garage, Station Road,
HETTON-LE-HOLE,
Tyne & Wear DH5 9JB.

Telephone: Hetton 262234

FLEET LIST

Date	Vehicle	Registration	Date	Vehicle	Registration
1919	Crossley charabanc	J 9135		Thornycroft Sturdy	HBB 578
1923	Ford Model T	PT 2367		Commer 3 ton tipper	HVK 144
1925	Crossley	PT 5270		Fordson 3 ton tipper	HVK 991
1926	Ford T wagon	PT 6607		Commer 4-5 ton tipper	JBB 216
1929	Morris	BR 7014	1940	Commer N5 tipper	EBB 608
	Ford	UP 3740		Commer N5 tipper	EVK 37
1930	Guy 30cwt.	UP 4310		Commer N4 tipper	CTN 802
1931	Ford 30cwt tipper	UP 3740	1941	Fordson tractor	EUP 433
1932	Morris Cattle Truck		1942	Commer 4-5 ton tipper	EUP 863
	Vulcan 2.5 ton	PT 8762	1942	Thornycroft Sturdy	JTN 279
	Bedford 2 tonner	BR 8878	1929	Thornycroft A1	TY 7368
1933	Chevrolet	FT 2390	1944	Muir-Hill shovel	FUP 351
	Morris	UP 2575	1945	Maudslay Mogul II	FUP 187
	Fordson 2 ton	UP 7620	1947	Thornycroft Sturdy	HUP 621
	Crossley Tractor	UP 4692	1950	Thornycroft Sturdy	LPT 461
	Vulcan tipper / cattle	WM 9430		Thornycroft tipper	LPT 462
1934	Reo Speedwagon	UP 8692		Chaseside shovel	JUP 137
	Commer Centaur	AVK 476	1952	Muir-Hill shovel	KPT 935
	Morris	UP 9518		Muir-Hill dumper	FPT 739
1935	Vulcan 30 cwt	VK 3874		Muir-Hill dumper	LPT 797
	Commer	APT 398		Muir-Hill dumper	LPT 798
	Morris	CN 3864		Muir-Hill dumper	LPT 799
	Morris 30cwt.	UP 2575		Muledozer	HUP 879
1936	Morris	VK 5480		Proctor	HUP 135
	Commer	DTN 949		Proctor	JPT 199
1937	Vulcan 50 cwt tipper	BFY 173	1953	Austin 5 ton tipper	OPT 558
	Dennis 25cwt	JR 2409		Thornycroft Sturdy	GUP 682
	Commer	EBB 719	1954	Commer 5-ton	GR 9671
1937	Commer LN5	EVK 496	1955	Thornycroft Sturdy	RPT 634
	Commer LN5	FBB 619	1956	Commer 5 ton	RTN 523
1938	Fordson 4-5 ton tipper	FTN 37	1957	Commer 7 ton QX	WPT 52
	Commer LN5 tipper	FVK 36	1958	Weatherill loading shovel	YPT
	Vulcan 2.5 tonner	APT 172	1957	Commer 7 ton QX	XTN 477
	Commer LN5 tipper	GTN 257		BMC coal wagon	OVN 229
	Guy	VK 4218	1959	Commer TS3	99 DPT
	Guy	VK 4219		Commer / Unipower 6w.	PBR 806
1939	Muir-Hill shovel	EPT 231	1960	Commer TS3	86 JPT

Date	Vehicle	Registration	Date	Vehicle	Registration
	Commer TS3 tipper	321 JPT		ERF C Series artic	B881 EDP
	Commer TS3 tipper	595 MTN	1993	Leyland Roadrunner	E268 ULS
1961	Commer 7 ton	415 PTN		Seddon Atkinson 401	B249 PHA
1962	Commer / Unipower 6w.	8730 PT	1994	Seddon Atkinson Strato	M111 ENR
	AEC Marshal six wheeler	124 UP		ERF E Series artic	F22 YUA
1963	Commer 8 ton	939 LUP		Leyland Roadrunner	E323 NDC
	Commer	VBR 319	1995	ERF E Series artic	H718 FLD
1967	AEC Marshal six wheeler	WUP 555F		ERF E Series artic	D629 VMO
	Commer	NBB 463E		ERF E Series artic	D625 VMO
	Commer	OUP 7D		ERF E Series artic	K195 JPW
1968	Commer TS3	345 SHN		ERF E Series artic	K956 JEX
1969	BMC Laird	DPT 977G		ERF E Series artic	H539 ERO
	AEC Mercury	GPT 70H	1996	Volvo FL10 4x2 unit	L452 GHN
1970	AEC Marshal six wheeler	KUP 8J		ERF EC14 4x2 unit	M383 NNC
1971	Leyland Boxer	NUP 29J		ERF EC artic unit	M618 MEE
1975	Leyland Marathon artic	JPT 848N	1997	ERF EC artic unit	P450 XBB
1976	ERF artic unit	RPT 499K	1999	ERF EC artic unit	V75 DFT
1977	ERF artic unit	UJR 927H		ERF EC artic unit	N643 JWR
	AEC Mandator artic	MPT 876J	2001	MAN 4x2 unit	S544 RAO
1978	Atkinson Borderer	PPT 733K		MAN 4x2 unit	S548 RAO
	Leyland Marathon	AVH 211R		MAN 4x2 unit	S568 RAO
1979	ERF B Series artic	RVH 948T	2002	MAN 7.5 tonne rigid	T519 BLM
1981	Ford D Series 4w.	GRG 117N		MAN 7.5 tonne rigid	MV 02 XPU
	ERF A Series artic	GJB 158N		MAN 7.5 tonne rigid	NU 02 KGG
1982	ERF C Series artic	SCU 427Y	2003	MAN 26.414 6x2 unit	V56 DNA
	Daf 2800 artic	YHN 381Y		MAN 26.414 6x2 unit	V86 DNA
1984	ERF B Series artic	MTY 212R		MAN 26.414 6x2 unit	V87 DNA
1986	ERF B Series artic	KYA 561T	2004	ERF ECS 6x2 unit	X797 CBT
	Leyland Chieftain	BCU 721V		ERF ECS 6x2 unit	X799 CBT
	Leyland Terrier rigid	A627 FGR	2005	Foden Alpha 6x2 unit	SV 05 FHX
1987	Leyland Freight Rover	PPY 666X			
1989	ERF E Series artic	F794 LTY			
	Dennis Dominant	NBB 905R			

IN PRESERVATION

Date	Vehicle	Registration
1990	ERF E Series artic	G338 VNL
	Leyland Freighter rigid	C541 DDB
	Foden Fleetmaster	EYR 23V
	Daf 2100 rigid	B866 BCP
1991	ERF 4x2 unit	D52 MKH
	Daf 3300 artic unit	B483 LVN
	Foden S104 artic unit	C467 XRF
	ERF B Series artic	GTY 800W

Date	Vehicle	Registration
1925	Morris Commercial charabanc	SV 8236
1930	Foden C type	RY 9259
1939	Thornycroft Sturdy	HBB 578
1945	Maudslay Mogul Mk II	FUP 187
1945	Scammell box tractor	DYS 319
1959	Commer / Unipower six wheeler	
		PBR 806
1972	AEC Mandator tractor unit	WHK 926L

E.&N. Ritchie Transport
Over 100 years of Service to Industry